Individual Choice and Social Welfare
Theoretical Foundations of Political Economy

A Research Literature Review

For a list of all Edward Elgar published titles visit our website at
www.e-elgar.com

Individual Choice and Social Welfare

Theoretical Foundations of Political Economy

A Research Literature Review

Viktor J. Vanberg

Professor Emeritus at The University of Freiburg
Member of the Board of the Walter Eucken Institut, Freiburg
Germany

Edward Elgar
Cheltenham, UK • Northampton, MA, USA

© Viktor J. Vanberg 2019

All rights reserved. No part of this publication may be reproduced, stored in a retrieval system, or transmitted in any form or by any means, electronic, mechanical, photocopying, recording, or otherwise without the prior permission of the publisher.

Published by
Edward Elgar Publishing Limited
The Lypiatts
15 Lansdown Road
Cheltenham
Glos GL50 2JA
UK

Edward Elgar Publishing, Inc.
William Pratt House
9 Dewey Court
Northampton
Massachusetts 01060
USA

A catalogue record for this book
is available from the British Library

This book is available electronically as an Elgar Research Literature Review in the ElgarOnline.com Economics Collection
DOI 10.4337/9781786432339

ISBN 978 1 83910 077 2 (paperback)
ISBN 978 1 78643 233 9 (eBook)

Printed and bound in Great Britain by TJ International Ltd, Padstow

Contents

About this Research Review

Elgar Research Literature Reviews offer an authoritative summary of the seminal works that have established a field of research. World-renowned experts research and select the most important readings in their field and provide a detailed essay outlining the evolution of these disciplines.

The *Literature Review* presented in this book was originally published as the introductory chapter to Professor Viktor J. Vanberg's Elgar Research Collection volume *Choice and Economic Welfare* (2019, ISBN 978 1 78643 232 2) and is also available electronically from Elgaronline.com (ISBN 978 1 78643 233 9).

The Recommended Readings following the *Review* have full references to faciliate further research.

It is important to note that the text printed in this book is identical to that in the printed Research Collection and the eBook.

Individual Choice and Social Welfare: Theoretical Foundations of Political Economy

Viktor J. Vanberg

1   Political Economy as Applied Economics

What we call an *economy*, that is, the nexus of economic activities and relations within some defined regional limits (e.g. a local, a national or the world economy), has always been subject to measures taken, or constraints imposed, by political authorities. How economies work is inevitably, and to a significant extent, contingent on the political environment within which they operate.

It is not surprising that economists studying the working principles of economic systems have rarely been content with confining their work to describing and explaining the economic realities they observe. Their ambitions always extended to passing judgments on the policies that shaped these realities and to providing guidance for what politics ought to do to improve economic matters.[1] In economics explanations of *what is* and judgments on what politics *should do* are often more closely intertwined than in most other fields of scientific inquiry, and more than from practitioners in other fields the general public expects economists to pass such policy judgments.

Political economy, the name under which economics originated, explicitly reflects the close connection of explanatory and policy concerns.[2] Adam Smith's *An Inquiry into the Nature and Causes of the Wealth of Nations* (1776), the founding treatise of modern economics, was as much a theoretical exposition of the principles governing economic activities as a critique of a policy he termed "mercantilism," charging it with serving the interests of the merchants' class rather than, as in his view it should, the interests of the citizenry at large.[3] As Smith put it, political economy, which he defined as "a branch of the science of a statesman or legislator" ([1776] 1981: 428), is about how "to increase the riches and the power of the country" (ibid.: 372).[4] Half a century later, echoing Adam Smith, Nassau William Senior (1827: 7) defined political economy as

> the science which teaches in what wealth consists … and what are the institutions and customs by which production may be facilitated and distribution regulated, so as to give the largest possible amount of wealth to each individual.

Being surely aware of David Hume's reminder that the logical gulf between statements about "what is" and statements about "what ought to be" does not allow them to simply deduce their policy judgments from their factual conjectures, economists faced the challenge to specify on what grounds they extend the authority they may claim for their scientific findings to the judgments they pass on policy issues.[5] Responding to this challenge, and commenting on Adam Smith's view of political economy as "a science which teaches, or professes to teach, in what manner a nation may be made rich," John Stuart Mill ([1844] 2006: 312) argued that such a definition

> seems liable to the conclusive objection, that it confounds the essentially distinct, though closely connected, ideas of *science* and *art*. These two ideas differ from one another as the understanding differs from the will, or as the indicative mood in grammar differs from the imperative. The one deals in facts, the other in precepts. Science is a collection of *truths*; art, a body of *rules*, or directions for conduct. The language of science is, This is, or, This is not; This does, or does not happen. The language of art is, Do this; Avoid that.

In their aspiration to establish their field of study as a "science" on equal footing with the natural sciences, economists put increasing emphasis on the separation between what they are concerned with in their role as scientists and policy issues. In the same vein as Mill, but in even stronger wording, Léon Walras ([1877] 1984: 51f., Chapter 1 in this volume) noted in reference to Adam Smith's definition of political economy "as a branch of the science of a statesman or legislator":

> [T]he distinguishing characteristic of a science is the complete indifference to consequences, good or bad, which it carries on the pursuit of pure truth. ... Thus, if political economy were simply what Adam Smith said it was ... it would certainly be a very interesting subject, but it would not be a science in the narrow sense of the term.

William Stanley Jevons, for whom, as for Walras, theoretical physics was the role model of a true science, explicitly stated that "it would be well to discard, as quickly as possible, the old troublesome double-worded name of our Science" (Jevons [1871] 1965: xiv), that is, political economy, and he expressed the hope "that *Economics* will become the recognized name of a science" (ibid.: xv).[6] It was only a natural consequence of the discipline's concerns for its recognition as a science, that by the late 19th century, symbolized by Alfred Marshall's textbook *Principles of Economics* (1890),[7] the name *political economy* was in fact discarded and replaced by *economics*.[8]

That the adjective *political* was eliminated from their field's name did not mean, though, that economists would no longer address policy issues, which would have meant, after all, giving up the claim that their theoretical findings are of practical-political relevance, a claim economists ostensibly wanted to uphold.[9] It meant, however, that they had to answer the challenge of how to reconcile this claim with the claim – symbolized by the renaming of the discipline – that theirs is a true science. Faced with the difficulty of answering this challenge, economists have occasionally suggested to divide the field in two parts, a *positive* economics satisfying the latter claim and a *normative* economics devoted to practical-political issues. This replaces, though, only one challenge by another, namely having to explain what kind of enterprise such a *normative* economics is supposed to be and on what authority it may pronounce its policy judgments.

John Stuart Mill addressed the above-noted issue in reference to political economy when, following his previously quoted argument, he stated:

> If, therefore, Political Economy be a science, it cannot be a collection of practical rules; though, unless it be altogether a useless science, practical rules must be capable of being founded upon it. The science of mechanics, a branch of natural philosophy, lays down the laws of motion, and the properties of what are called the mechanical powers. The art of practical mechanics teaches how we may avail ourselves of those laws and properties, to increase our command over external nature. ... Rules, therefore, for making a nation increase in wealth, are not a science, but they are the results of science. Political Economy does not of itself instruct how to make a nation rich; but whoever would be qualified to judge of the means of making a nation rich, must first be a political economist (Mill [1844] 2006: 312).

The answer to the challenge of reconciling the demands of a science with the claim of practical relevance that Mill implies is essentially what Senior (1827: 7f.) had suggested before, namely, that

> the science of Political Economy may be divided into two great branches – the theoretic and the practical. The first or theoretic branch ... explains the nature, production, and distribution of wealth. ... The practical branch of the science, that of which the office is to ascertain what institutions are most favorable to wealth, is a far more arduous study.

In a similar vein Léon Walras ([1874] 1984: 57, Chapter 1 in this volume) proposed to "divide political economy into a natural science, a moral science and an art" or applied science,[10] noting that the "distinguishing characteristics" or the "respective *criteria*" of science, art and ethics are "the *true*; the *useful*, meaning material well-being; and the *good*, meaning justice" (ibid.: 64).

Yet, the various proposals for separating the "scientific" branch of economics, that is, the branch that bans from its domain all value judgments, from its "applied" or "art" branches still faces the challenge of specifying the role that in the latter branches value judgments may play, and what the inclusion of such judgments means for their status as parts of an inclusively defined discipline of economics. The ambiguities that have surrounded, and still surround, much of the profession's debate on this issue[11] can be avoided by simply distinguishing between two kinds of value judgments or should-statements, namely *hypothetical* or *conditional* imperatives on the one hand and *categorical* or *unconditional* imperatives on the other. Categorical value judgments are of the form "X should be done," hypothetical value judgments are of the form "X should be done if one wants to achieve Y."[12] Occasionally, if only rarely, this distinction and its relevance for the value-judgment problem is explicitly recognized in discussions on the status of political economy, as, for instance, when Hennipman (1992: 429f.) states in reference to welfare economics:

> In consequence, the positive theory does not aim at offering categorical policy prescriptions, it only gives recommendations that are conditional on the acceptance of the postulated goal. They are, in

more weighty wording, hypothetical imperatives. ... This simple scheme definitely refutes the view that welfare economics is necessarily normative because it "deals with policy."[13]

While the "recommendations for policy" that an applied economics can provide are necessarily *based* on normative premises, the recommendations themselves are *hypothetical imperatives* that make purely factual claims; claims that can be subjected to the same kind of critical examination on empirical and theoretical grounds to which positive scientific statements are generally subjected. They are, as noted above, statements of the form "If X is aimed at, Y should be done" or "If problem A is to be solved, B should be done," statements that can be proven wrong if Y is in fact not a suitable means for achieving X, or B not a suitable means for solving A, or that can be shown to be insufficient if other means exist for achieving X or for solving A. Such hypothetical imperatives are, to be sure, of interest only for addressees who actually want to know how X may be achieved or A be solved.

In other words, a political economy conceived as applied economics, an economics applied to policy issues, can be practiced as an entirely value-free, positive scientific enterprise, even if it cannot but start from *hypothetically presumed* value premises that define the problem for which it seeks solutions and that limit the scope of its application.[14] The hypothetically presumed value premise that a political economist chooses to adopt provides the focus for his or her research efforts, the criterion for deciding which one from the unlimited number of potential issues merits to be addressed.[15] But it does not need to "infect" at all the products of these efforts, which can be entirely limited to factual claims.[16] It will mean, though, as indicated, that the research effort and its fruits will be of interest only to those who consider the chosen value premise a worthwhile guide for scientific inquiry.

Issuing hypothetical imperatives is the ordinary business of any applied science. In this regard, political economy conceived as applied economics is not different from applied disciplines in the natural sciences whose status as value-free scientific enterprises is unquestioned.[17] It may be looked at as being what Myrdal ([1922] 1953: 199) refers to as "economic technology," noting:

> Such an economic technology is in the best tradition of political economy, which has always aimed at social policy. It would have to become more relativistic, i.e. it would have to be related to explicit and concrete value premises.

The term *political economy* will be used here in this very sense, as a label for an applied economics, an economics that examines policy issues under the presumption that a hypothesized normative standard serves as measuring rod.[18]

2   Economics and Normative Individualism: Utility- or Preference-Individualism vs. Choice-Individualism

As explained above, political economy conceived as applied economics can be practiced as an analytical, scientific enterprise, proposing hypothetical imperatives that can be critically examined according to the standards generally applied in scientific discourse. Such a political economy, to be sure, can embark on its positive analytical task only after a normative premise is hypothetically presumed at the meta-theoretical level, be it a normative criterion against which policy measures are to be judged, a problem that politics is supposed to solve, or an aim it is assumed to pursue. Accordingly, in examining economic approaches that deal with policy issues, the first question to be asked concerns the normative standard the respective authors apply when passing judgments on the merits of alternative policies. Even if authors do not explicitly consider the normative standards they suppose as hypothetical criteria in the sense defined, which, in fact, they most often do not, their normative assumption can, as I suppose, be readily so re-interpreted. With such re-interpretation, the respective approaches can be looked at as pronouncing *factual* claims about what can be said *if* a particular normative standard is presupposed. This is the spirit in which I shall proceed in what follows.

As far as the normative premises are concerned with which they approach policy issues, economists appear to share widely a *normative individualism* in the sense that they judge policies in terms of their effects on individuals' well-being or, in other terms, that they take the evaluations of the individuals involved as the relevant standard for assessing policy measures.[19] As Kenneth Arrow (1987: 124) has put it:

> It has been granted in virtually all economic policy discussions since the time of Adam Smith, if not before, that alternative policies should be judged on the basis of their consequences for individuals.[20]

Likewise, P. Samuelson (1947: 223, Chapter 6 in this volume) has stressed the role played in economists' outlook on policy issues by the "assumption, which stems from the individualistic philosophy of modern Western Civilization … that individuals' preferences are to count."

The premise of normative individualism has, in fact, been so dominant in the tradition of political economy and is so widely shared among economic contributions to policy issues that it is justified to confine the discussion, as is done in the present volume, to approaches that fall into this rubric.[21] Such approaches, interpreted as exercises in applied economics, can be looked at as an attempt to explicate what can be said about economic and policy issues *if one presumes* that the individuals' evaluations provide the relevant normative standard.

As much as economists appear to agree on a normative individualism as the premise in their treatment of policy issues, on closer examination it can be shown that they interpret this premise in two critically different ways, namely, as I propose to call them, as *utility-* or *preference-* individualism on the one hand and *choice-individualism* on the other. While both versions of a normative individualism posit that the evaluations of the individuals involved should be taken as the measuring rod against which alternative policies are to be assessed, they differ in how they specify this measuring rod.

Under the rubric *utility-* or *preference-individualism* I shall classify approaches to policy issues that take individuals' utilities or preferences as the components from which the measuring rod is to be derived or, in other words, that interpret the premise that individuals' evaluations are to count as "individuals' utilities or preferences are to count." The paradigmatic example of this version of a normative individualism is Jeremy Bentham's utilitarianism, the central claim of which he circumscribes as follows:

> By the principle of utility is meant that principle which approves or disapproves of every action, whatever, according to the tendency which it appears to have to augment or diminish the happiness

of the party whose interest is in question ... not only of every action of a private individual, but of every measure of government. ... The community is a fictitious body, composed of the individual persons who are considered as constituting as it were its members. The interest of the community then is what? – the sum of the interests of the several members who compose it (Bentham [1789] 1982: 11f., Chapter 4 in this volume).

According to this concept, what actions government should take should be assessed by determining the net effects potential policy measures are predicted to have on individuals' utilities, and by aggregating the resulting individual utility measures across the community (ibid.: 39f.).[22]

In Bentham's utilitarian individualism the "members" of the community count only with their utility values; they need not be actively involved in political decision-making, since their utility values are supposedly assessed by the analyst doing the utility-accounting for the community. In other words, from such a perspective, utilities can conceptually be identified independently of any real act of choice. It is in the same spirit that, about hundred years after Bentham's pronouncement, Léon Walras ([1874] 1984: 256) stated in his founding treatise of neoclassical economics:

> In our theory each trader is assumed to determine his own utility or want curves as he pleases. Once these curves have been determined, we show how prices result from them under a hypothetical régime of absolutely free competition.

Vilfredo Pareto, Walras' successor on the Lausanne chair, stated likewise: "once we have determined the means at the disposal of the individual and obtained a 'photograph' of his tastes ... the individual may disappear."[23]

And in reference to the current practice in economics, Robert Sugden (2004: 1017) notes:

> It is a folk saying in the discipline that, as far as theory is concerned, an individual is a preference ordering: everything the theorist needs to know about a person is contained in that person's preference.

By contrast, from a *choice-individualist* perspective the normative premise that individuals' evaluations are to count in the assessment of policy measures is interpreted to mean that individuals' *choices*, rather than their utilities or preferences, are to be respected as the relevant input in political choice processes. The hypothetical criterion of evaluation on which a choice-individualist political economy bases its analysis is that "individual persons are the ultimate decision-makers" (Buchanan [1968] 2000: 4), that they "are the ultimate source of evaluation" (Buchanan [1985] 2001: 245), or, stated in yet another way, it is "the normative premise that individuals are the ultimate sovereigns in matters of social organization" (Buchanan [1991] 1999: 288). From such a perspective the measuring rod for policy choices is not to be constructed from individuals' utilities or preferences; it is to be derived from their *actual choices*.

The difference between the two versions of a normative individualism has significant implications for the direction into which economists' research efforts are guided, and for the nature of the theories they propose in order to bridge the gap between the level of individuals' evaluations and the level of policy choices. A main difference is that utility- or preference-individualism directs attention to the *outcomes* of policy choices, judging them in terms of the utilities or preferences of the individuals involved, while choice-individualism directs attention to the *procedures* through which policies are chosen, judging them in terms of how they translate individuals' choices into policy choices.

The principal research issues a utility- or preference-individualist approach faces are, firstly, how to determine individuals' utilities or preferences and, secondly, how to aggregate or combine them into a measure of "social utility" or "social preference." The predicted *outcomes* of policy choices are the *direct* object of evaluation, the procedures through which choices come about are only *indirectly* evaluated in terms of their capacity to generate valued outcomes.[24] For a choice-individualist approach the principal research issue is how collective, political choices can be derived from, or grounded in, the choices of the individuals who constitute the polity.[25] The *choice procedures* are the *direct* object of evaluation, judged in terms of their capacity to enable individuals to exercise their authority as ultimate sovereigns, while *policy outcomes* are judged only *indirectly* in terms of the nature of the procedure from which they result.

Utility- or preference-individualism has quite obviously been the dominant normative premise on which, influenced by Bentham's utilitarianism, economists who concerned themselves with policy issues founded their arguments. It provides the basis for welfare economics and social choice theory as the discipline's subfields explicitly devoted to these issues. The choice-individualist perspective has always been present in economic discourse, yet it remained mostly an implicit concept that has rarely been given noteworthy attention. It is only quite recently that it has found its explicit and systematic elaboration in the research program of constitutional political economy pioneered by James M. Buchanan.

The main subject of this volume and of the remainder of this introduction is a comparison of the three versions of the three research programs – welfare economics, social choice theory and constitutional political economy – focusing on how their respective foundation in a utility-individualist, a preference-individualist and a choice-individualist perspective shapes the research agendas that they pursue. As concerns this comparison, it should be kept in mind that these versions of a normative individualism are interpreted here as hypothesized *normative premises* on which the three research programs are based; premises that define the condition under which the conjectures they pronounce about policy issues are claimed to be valid. Naturally, as hypothesized normative criteria at the meta-theoretical level, neither utility- nor preference-individualism, nor choice-individualism, can be proven "right" or "wrong." They can only be judged in terms of their "fruits," that is, in terms of the fertility and relevance of the research agendas they give rise to. It is in this sense that the following comparison between the three research programs under review will be carried out. They will be compared in terms of how successful they are in yielding – starting from individuals' evaluations – a measuring rod against which public policies can be evaluated, and in terms of how relevant these measuring rods appear for informing actual political decision-making. From such a perspective, *welfare economics* is to be looked at as a research program that explores what can be said about policy measures *if* individuals' *utilities* are taken as the relevant normative criterion. *Social choice theory* is understood as a research program that explores what can be said about policy measures *if* individuals' *preferences* provide the measuring rod. *Constitutional political economy* is presented as a research program that explores what can be said about politics if individuals' choices provide the standard for evaluative judgments.

3   The Utility-Individualism of Welfare Economics

Utilitarian moral philosophy is generally considered to have "constituted the basis of economic thought" (Myrdal [1922] 1953: 8, Chapter 2 in this volume) in its early stages,[26] and it can be said to have had an enduring influence on economists' outlook on their subject matter, in particular their treatment of policy issues.[27] This is notably true of *welfare economics*,[28] the subfield in economics to which the practical-political concerns of classical political economy have been delegated[29] since, as noted above, economists renamed their discipline to *economics* in order to stress its nature as a purely theoretical science.[30] As Amartya Sen (1996: 21) has put it:

> Utilitarianism has been the "official" theory of welfare economics in a peculiarly unique way, and a good deal of standard welfare economics is still largely utilitarian. Even when the approach used is not fully utilitarian, it tends to incorporate central features of utilitarianism, such as exclusive reliance on utility information to evaluate social states (what has been called "welfarism") and exclusive reliance on the evaluation of the goodness of social states to assess actions, institutions and other choice variables (what is called "consequentialism").[31]

The three "utilitarian" features of welfare economics Sen points to are the very features that are of particular interest when comparing and contrasting its utility-individualism with a choice- individualist perspective, a comparison to which the present study wants to draw attention. These three features are, firstly, that *individual utilities* serve as normative reference points, secondly, that *social states* are considered the principal object of evaluation and, thirdly, that choice procedures, rules and institutions are evaluated only *indirectly* in terms of the *outcomes* they bring about.

   According to the utility-individualist normative premise of welfare economics – here viewed as the hypothetical criterion on which it is based in its interpretation as applied political economy – the "goodness of states of affairs must be judged exclusively by the individual utilities in the respective states" (Sen 1996: 22).[32] Throughout the history of their discipline, economists widely shared the general notion that individuals' own *evaluations* provide the criterion in terms of which policy choices should be judged. Yet, in welfare economics this was narrowed down to the notion that individual *utilities* are to be viewed as a normative standard, and was then further specified as the tenet that as a measure of an individual's evaluation one may "use his utility function (which represents his preferences)" (Ng 1979: 2) in social welfare assessments. As Atkinson (2009: 800) notes:

> The standard welfare economic approach is to assume that the domains are reduced to a single number representing individual welfare or utility, and the aggregation issue involves combining these into a single overall level of social welfare.

The welfarist reference to individual utilities as the criterion of evaluation has always been surrounded, though, by a certain ambiguity, blurring the critical difference between a utility-individualist and a choice-individualist paradigm. This ambiguity is apparent when Graaff in his much acclaimed *Theoretical Welfare Economics*[33] notes:

Attempts have often been made … to give objective meaning to a person's "welfare". … [F]or quite a long time the economist's conception has in any case been a subjective one. Something to the effect that welfare is a state of mind, or that "the elements of welfare are states of mind" is generally accepted. We shall accept it too; but we shall try to maintain an element of objectivity by linking individual welfare very closely to individual choice.

The matter can be put somewhat formally by saying that a person's welfare map is defined to be identical with his preference map which indicates how he would choose between different situations, if he were given the opportunity for choice (Graaff [1963] 1968: 4f.).

In equating a person's "hypothetical choice function" with his "*utility* function" (ibid.: 34),[34] Graaff in effect only renames the latter; he does not thereby add, as he appears to impute, an "element of objectivity" to the concept of *welfare*.[35] Obviously, the observing economist can have no more direct knowledge of what a person *would choose* than he can of the person's *subjective utilities*. There remains, accordingly, a fundamental difference between a welfare economics that takes its departure from individual utility functions describing *hypothetical choices* and a choice-individualist approach that takes its departure from individuals' *actual choices*.

3.1   The "Old," Utilitarian Welfare Economics

Arthur C. Pigou, whose treatise *The Economics of Welfare* (1920) is generally credited for having given the subfield of welfare economics its name,[36] is generally regarded as the principal representative of the so-called "old," utilitarian welfare economics.[37] Pigou considered his efforts as a project in applied economics; a project motivated not by "the philosopher's impulse, knowledge for the sake of knowledge, but rather the physiologist's, knowledge for the healing that knowledge may help to bring" (Pigou [1920] 1932: 5).[38] Though motivated by ethical concerns the project itself was in his view a contribution to "positive economics"; he remained, however, ambiguous about how the logical gulf was supposed to be bridged.[39] As he noted:

If this conception of the motive behind economic study is accepted, it follows that the type of science that the economist will endeavor to develop must be one adapted to form the basis of an art. It will not, indeed, itself be an art, or directly enunciate precepts of government. It is a positive science of what is and tends to be, not a normative science of what ought to be. … But, though wholly independent in its tactics and its strategy, it will be guided in general direction by practical interests. … The goal sought is to make more easy practical measures to promote welfare – practical measures which statesmen may build upon the work of the economist (Pigou [1920] 1932: 5, 10).

In studying *welfare*, the promotion of which he considers the task of politics, Pigou starts from two "more or less dogmatically" laid down propositions,

First, that the elements of welfare are states of consciousness and, perhaps their relations; secondly, that welfare can be brought under the category of greater and less (ibid.: 10).

That welfare is about "states of consciousness," or, in other words, a subjective variable about which the observing economist can have no direct knowledge, means, Pigou concluded, that it is "necessary to limit our subject matter" (ibid.: 11). This limitation he thus specifies:

> In doing this we are naturally attracted toward that portion of the field in which the methods of science seem likely to work at best advantage. This they can clearly do when there is present something measurable, on which analytical machinery can get a first grip. The one obvious instrument of measurement available in social life is money. Hence, the range of our inquiry becomes restricted to that part of social welfare that can be brought directly or indirectly into relation with the measuring- rod of money (ibid.).

Pigou recognizes that the limitation to a so-defined *economic* welfare may create problems for the "practical usefulness of our conclusions" (ibid.: 12) because, so he notes, "our ultimate interest is, of course, in the effects which the various causes investigated are likely to have upon welfare as a whole" (ibid.: 11f.). Yet, while admitting that "any rigid inference from effects on economic welfare to effects on total welfare is out of the question" (ibid.: 20), he still feels justified in claiming:

> When we have ascertained the effects of any cause on economic welfare, we may, unless of course, there is specific evidence to the contrary, regard this effect as probably equivalent in direction, though not in magnitude to the effect on total welfare (ibid.).

And he concludes:

> The above result suggests *prima facie* that economic science, when it shall have come to full development, is likely to furnish a powerful guide to practice (ibid.).

Whether economic welfare or *wealth* can count as a meaningful criterion in guiding politics had long been a subject of debate ever since Adam Smith in his *Inquiry into the Nature and Causes of the Wealth of Nations* spoke of wealth as an indicator of "the general welfare of the society" ([1776] 1981: 22).[40] Nassau William Senior had commented on this debate:

> With respect to the first of these obstacles, it has often been made a matter of grave complaint against Political Economists, that they confine their attention to Wealth, and disregard all consideration of Happiness or Virtue. It is to be wished that this complaint were better founded; but its general existence implies an opinion that it is the business of Political Economists not merely to state propositions, but to recommend actual measures; for on no other supposition could they be blamed for confining their attention to a single subject. No one blames a writer upon tactics for confining his attention to military affairs, or, from his doing so, infers that he recommends perpetual war. It must be admitted that an author who, having stated that a given conduct is productive of Wealth, should, on that account alone, recommend it, or assume that, on that account alone, it ought to be pursued, would be guilty of the absurdity of implying that Happiness and the possession of Wealth are identical. But his error would consist not in confining his attention to Wealth, but in confounding Wealth with Happiness (Senior 1836: 130).

Senior's statement is a reminder that an applied political economy must hypothesize some normative criterion and that the hypothetical imperatives it pronounces are contingent on the acceptance of this criterion. It is, accordingly, not objectionable for a political economy to focus on economic welfare or wealth as its criterion; what is objectionable is to tacitly shift the meaning of this criterion by suggesting that – as a variable that supposedly can be objectively measured – it can serve as proxy for general welfare, which is acknowledged to be a subjective magnitude.[41] When this shift in meaning is combined with the claim that propositions about what fosters wealth are purely positive conjectures, it is made to appear as if *positive* economics can directly recommend welfare-advancing policies, concealing as factual claims what are in fact value judgments.

That it conceals the normative character of its claims has been a principal objection against the "old," utilitarian welfare economics to which Pigou had given its name and most comprehensive exposition. This critique was, in terms of its impact in the profession, most effectively voiced by Lionel Robbins in his *An Essay on the Nature and Significance of Economic Science* (1932), a critique that Gunnar Myrdal ([1922] 1953) had similarly voiced a decade before, receiving, though, little attention.[42] With his critique Robbins targeted in particular the utilitarian tenet that social welfare is to be determined as the sum total of the welfares or utilities experienced by the individual members of the respective community,[43] a tenet that Pigou expressed in these terms:

> The economic welfare of a community consists in the balance of satisfaction derived from the use of the national dividend over the dissatisfaction involved in the making of it (Pigou [1920] 1932: 85).[44]

Such a claim, Robbins charged, presumes that individual utilities are cardinally measurable and comparable across persons,[45] a claim that cannot be upheld in light of the purely *subjective* nature of the entries in the supposed summation. As he put it:

> It is a comparison which necessarily falls outside the scope of any positive science. To state that A's preference stands above B's in order of importance is entirely different from stating that A prefers *n* to *m* and B prefers *n* and *m* in a different order. It involves an element of conventional valuation. Hence it is essentially normative. It has no place in pure science (Robbins 1932: 123, Chapter 3 in this volume).

About half a century later he restated his criticism in these terms:

> The *raison d'être* of Welfare Economics is simple. How desirable it would be if we were able to pronounce as a matter of scientific demonstration that such and such a policy was good or bad. ... But as soon as we move to the plane of welfare, we introduce elements which are not of that order. As in the great work of Marshall and, still more, Pigou we are assuming ... comparisons between the satisfactions and dissatisfactions of the different persons involved. And that, I would urge, is not warranted by anything which is legitimately assumed by scientific economics (Robbins 1981: 4f., Chapter 13 in this volume).[46]

Robbins' argument is, though, not without ambiguity because he tacitly conflates two different objections, namely, on the one hand, that interpersonal comparisons of utility *cannot be made* and, on the other hand, that such comparisons amount to value judgments.[47] His principal objection against the utilitarian construction appears to be that it ignores the logical gulf between statements about "what is" and statements about "what ought to be," thereby violating the postulate of value-free science.[48] Yet, it is not at all clear what role the issue of the interpersonal comparison of utilities is meant to play in his argument. Whether such comparison is possible or not is a factual matter, and whether one claims that it is or that it is not has per se no normative connotation. A value judgment is introduced only by claiming that the aggregation of individual utilities based on such a comparison should be the criterion on which policy choices are to be made.[49] Even if such aggregation were possible, adopting it as a criterion for policy choices would still involve a value judgment.[50] Naturally, if such aggregation is not possible, a welfare economics based on the premise of interpersonal comparability loses its foundation.[51]

As argued above, Robbins' charge that satisfaction or utility cannot be interpersonally compared can be, and must be, separated from the charge that the utilitarian construction violates the postulate of value-free science.[52] Clearly to distinguish between these two charges could have helped to avoid some of the confusion that has clouded the discussion prompted by Robbins' critique.[53] What would have also helped to clarify matters would have been an explicit recognition of the proper role played by value judgments in welfare economics as *applied* science: that the utilitarian welfare concept serves as a *hypothetical* criterion providing the focus for the conditional or hypothetical imperatives conjectured on this basis. Robbins himself points to the possibility of resolving the value-judgment problem by such re-interpretation of welfare-economic claims when he comments in retrospect on his criticism:

> All economists recognized that their prescriptions regarding policy were conditional upon the acceptance of norms lying outside economics. All that I was doing was only to recognize that, in a field of generalizations hitherto thought to involve no normative elements, there were in fact such elements concealed. The traditional political economy, for instance, had taught that free trade increased social wealth. It had fully recognized that the prescription, built on the analysis, that free was a good thing, was contingent on the assumption that an increase of wealth was to be desired (Robbins 1938: 638).[54]

Explicitly recognizing that in welfare economics as an applied science value judgments need to play a role only as a hypothetical criterion of evaluation could, for instance, have helped Samuelson to state with greater clarity his comments on Robbins' position:

> In practice, if pushed to extremes, this somewhat schizophrenic rule [of value-free science] becomes difficult to adhere to, and it leads to rather tedious circumlocutions. But in essence, Robbins is undoubtedly correct. ... But it is not valid to conclude from this that there is no room in economics for what goes under the name of "welfare economics." It is a legitimate exercise of economic analysis to examine the consequences of various value judgments, whether or not they are shared by the theorist, just as the study of comparative ethics is itself a science like any other branch of anthropology. ... It is only fair to point out, however, that the theorems enunciated under the heading of welfare economics are not meaningful propositions of hypotheses in the technical

sense. For they represent the deductive implications of assumptions which are not themselves meaningful refutable hypotheses about reality (Samuelson 1947: 220f., Chapter 6 in this volume).

In any event, notwithstanding the ambiguity of its charge, Robbins' critique of the utilitarian proposal for measuring social or collective welfare had a lasting impact in the profession, and it is commonly portrayed as having terminated the era of the "old" welfare economics,[55] as vividly depicted by Paul Samuelson:

> When Robbins sang out that the emperor had no clothes – that you could not prove or test by any empirical observations of objective science the normative validity of comparisons between different persons' utilities – suddenly all his generation of economists felt themselves to be naked in a cold world. Most of them had come into economics seeking the good. To learn in midlife that theirs was only the craft of a plumber, dentist, or cost accountant was a sad shock (Samuelson 1981: 226).

3.2 The "New," Paretian Welfare Economics

As the utilitarian supposition of cardinal utility had to be given up and it became the dominant view that utility can only be measured in *ordinal* terms, ruling out interpersonal comparisons,[56] concerns were voiced in the profession that such resignation would mean to give up the ambition, considered to be a central part of the economist's mission, to judge policy issues, a concern Harrod stated thus in an influential article:

> It is not altogether certain that the gulf between the prescriptions of the classical economists and those of, shall I call them, the welfare school is as great as Professor Robbins implies. ... Consider the Repeal of the Corn Laws. This tended to reduce the value of a specific factor of production – land. It can no doubt be shown that the gain to the community as a whole exceeded the loss of the landlords – but only if individuals are treated in some sense as equal. ... If the incomparability of utility to different individuals is strictly pressed, not only are the prescriptions of the welfare school ruled out, but all prescriptions whatever. The economist as an advisor is completely stultified (Harrod 1938: 396f.).[57]

Given the limitations dictated by a purely ordinal concept of utility, but not wanting to give up the claim to practical-political relevance, economists looked for ways to arrive at welfare judgments that would allow one to pass judgment on policies. These possibilities, one hoped, could be found in a criterion Vilfredo Pareto had stated several decades earlier in his *Trattato Di Sociologia Generale*, namely that a change that makes at least one person better off without making anybody else worse off can unequivocally be judged socially desirable. What he called the criterion of "maximum ophelimity" Pareto described in these words:

> When the community stands at a point, Q, that it can leave with resulting benefits to all individuals, procuring greater enjoyment for all of them, it is obvious that from the economic standpoint it is advisable not to stop at that point, but to move on from it as far as the movement away from it is advantageous to all. When, then, the point P, where that is no longer possible, is reached, it is necessary, as regards the advisability of stopping there or going on, to resort to other considerations

foreign to economics – to decide on grounds of ethics, social utility, or something else, which individuals it is advisable to benefit, which to sacrifice (Pareto [1916] 1935: §2129).[58]

When Pareto suggests that his criterion for judging social changes can be posited from "the strictly economic standpoint" in contrast to criteria "foreign to economics," he seems to imply that it is compatible with economics as a positive science. Yet, if it is meant, as Pareto says, to inform about what is "advisable," it implies doubtlessly a value judgment, albeit one that as a derivative of a normative individualism enjoys broad acceptance in the profession as the hypothetical norm on which political economy as applied science is based.[59]

That a value judgment is implied when what has come to be named *Pareto optimality*[60] is supposed to serve as a criterion for judging policies is often not recognized, presumably because it appears to be self-evident.[61] Its perception as an uncontroversial standard of judgment finds support in the common practice of treating the Pareto criterion as equivalent to a unanimity criterion, a practice exemplified

- when Samuelson (1981: 224) speaks in reference to it of "a movement from the status quo which by unanimity could make everyone better off,"
- when Sen (1987: 382) describes it as "demanding that unanimous individual preferences over any pair of states should yield the corresponding social preference over that state," or
- when Baujard (2016: 615) states that it "implies unanimity to justify any change."[62]

Apart from the fact that equating it with "unanimity" cannot alter the normativity of the Pareto criterion as a standard for what is "advisable," treating the two as equivalent means to pass over the paradigmatic divide between the two versions of a normative individualism that are contrasted in this study. As defined by its author and as commonly used, the Pareto criterion belongs clearly under the rubric of a *utility- or preference-individualism*. It is meant to be used by the observer-economist in assessing how social policies affect the well-being of the individuals concerned. It is meant to serve as a tool for a research agenda that explores what can be said about policy issues if one takes as hypothetical norm "that individuals' *preferences* are to 'count'" (Samuelson 1947: 223, Chapter 6 in this volume, my emphasis). To be sure, as I shall discuss later (section 5), the Pareto criterion can be re-interpreted as a unanimity criterion within a choice-individualist framework. But, so re-interpreted it becomes part of a categorically different research agenda, one that explores what can be said about policy issues if one starts from the premise that individual *choices* are to count.

Within the utility- or preference-individualist framework the Pareto criterion helped to avoid the charges leveled against the "old," utilitarian welfare economics, but it came with an obvious drawback of its own. As its author had already pointed out, its range of applicability is severely limited: what is advisable, it only can say in the case of policies that are "advantageous to all." In the case of policies that make some members of the community better off but others worse off – in other words, in the case of distributional consequences – it remains silent.[63] Since it can be rarely expected that policy measures have literally no negative consequences for anybody, the Pareto criterion will thus only be applicable in the rarest of cases.[64] The two branches of the so-called *New Welfare Economics* that were built on the

Pareto criterion,[65] the Kaldor–Hicks "compensation school" and the Bergson–Samuelson welfare function-approach, sought to remedy this shortcoming using different means.

3.2.1   THE KALDOR–HICKS "COMPENSATION SCHOOL"

Reacting to Harrod's (1938: 397) worry that, if "the comparability of utility of different individuals is strictly pressed ... the economist as adviser is completely stultified," Nicolas Kaldor published a brief note in which he argued:

> In all cases, therefore, where a certain policy leads to an increase in physical productivity, and thus of aggregate real income, the economist's case for the policy is quite unaffected by the question of the comparability of individual satisfaction; since in all such cases it is *possible* to make everybody better off than before, or at any rate to make some people better off without making anybody worse off. There is no need for the economist to prove – as indeed he never could prove – that as a result of the adoption of a certain measure nobody in the community is going to suffer. In order to establish his case, it is quite sufficient for him to show that even if all those who suffer are fully compensated for their loss, the rest of the community will still be better off than before (Kaldor 1939: 550).

Apparently inspired by and shortly after Kaldor's note, John R. Hicks (1939: 696, Chapter 5 in this volume) addressed the issue of "the proper attitude of economists towards economic policy" in a paper on "The Foundations of Welfare Economics," stating:

> During the nineteenth century, it was generally considered to be the business of an economist, not only to explain the economic world ..., but also to lay down principles of economic policy, to say what policies are likely to be conducive to social welfare ... Today, there is one school of writers which continue to claim that economics can fulfill this second function, but there is another which (formally at least) desires to reject it. According to their view the economics of welfare, the economics of economic policy, is too unscientific in character to be a part of economic science. ... It cannot be denied that the latter view is in fact widely accepted. ... But it is rather a dreadful thing to have to accept. No one will question the activity of some of our "positivists" ... but ... economic positivism might easily become an excuse for the shirking of life issues, very conducive to the euthanasia of our science (ibid.: 696f.).

Pointing to "the difficulty of inter-personal comparisons" and the fact that there is "not a single system of ends, but as many independent systems as there are 'individuals' in the community" (ibid.: 699), Hicks notes that this "appears to introduce a hopeless arbitrariness" (ibid.) in judging the merits of policy measures. As he puts it:

> You cannot take a temperature when you have to use, not one thermometer, but an immense number of different thermometers, working on different principles, and with no necessary correlation between their registrations (ibid.).

Of the three possible ways Hicks considers for dealing with this difficulty he rejects two. One is "to replace the given thermometer (the scales of preferences of the individuals) by a new thermometer of one's own" (ibid.) – which would amount to abandoning the premise of normative individualism on which the welfarist project had been based in the first place. The other is to "seek for some way of aggregating the reports of the different thermometers" (ibid.: 700), a project that Pigou and others had pursued but that had proven to be impossible. As the third, and promising, avenue, Hicks takes up Kaldor's suggestion to concentrate attention on those cases in which it is possible to compensate, with a net advantage left, the losers of policy measures.[66] In summarizing his argument Hick's states:

> By adopting the line of analysis set out in this paper, it is possible to put welfare economics on a secure basis, and to render it immune from positivist criticism. … The main practical advantage of our line of approach is that it fixes attention upon the question of compensation. Every simple economic reform inflicts a loss upon some people; the reforms we have studied are marked out by the characteristic that they will allow of compensation to balance that loss, and they will still show a net advantage (1939: 711, Chapter 5 in this volume).

It did not take long, though, for the Kaldor–Hicks compensation test to come under attack from critics, such as, in particular, Scitovsky (1941), who exposed its shortcomings. In the present context, which is concerned with the general conceptual issues raised by the utility-individualist foundation of welfare economics, there is no need to discuss the "technical criticism or correction" (Samuelson 1958: 540) that Scitovsky and others have voiced.[67] Of relevance in the present context is the discussion of whether the Kaldor–Hicks compensation test requires that compensation is actually paid or only that it could hypothetically be paid. Kaldor (1939: 550f.) had stated his view on this matter as follows:

> Whether the landlord, in the free trade case, should in fact be given compensation or not, is a political question on which the economist, *qua* economist, could hardly pronounce an opinion. The important fact is that, in the argument in favor of free trade, the fate of the landlords is wholly irrelevant: since the benefits of free trade are by no means destroyed even if the landlords are fully reimbursed for their losses.

In a similar vein Hicks (1939: 711, Chapter 5 in this volume) argued:

> I do not contend that there is any ground for saying that compensation ought always to be given; whether or not compensation should be given in any particular case is a question of distribution, upon which there cannot be identity of interest, and so there cannot be any generally acceptable principle.

Given the *subjective* nature of satisfaction, critics have pointed out that welfare judgments derived from assessments of whether compensation could *hypothetically* be paid rest on dubious foundations. Baumol (1946: 45) called it a crucial weakness of the compensation test that "it does require that persons injured by some economic phenomenon must *actually be compensated* in full by those who have gained from it" and elaborated:

> Are we justified in assuming that because the money measure of a gain to one set of individuals is greater than the money measure of the loss to a *different* set of individuals that society as a whole has indeed benefited? To take a crude illustration, let us assume that all the persons who gain from

an innovation are very rich whereas all the losers are in a highly impoverished state. Is it then reasonable to assume that the subjective value of money does not vary from one group to the other? … Indeed, it seems very likely that the same amount of money might well represent a much greater loss to the poorer group than the corresponding gain to the richer (ibid.).[68]

As for other critics, Little (1957: 93) simply stated that "hypothetical compensation is not a method of finding anything out" and Robbins (1981: 6, Chapter 13 in this volume) argued that "the fact that such compensation is *conceivable* is not sufficient: if it is not actual, the fundamental Paretian condition is violated." In fact, Hicks (1939: 711, Chapter 5 in this volume) indirectly acknowledges the limits of hypothetical compensation when he notes about economic reforms that would pass this test:

> Yet, when such reforms have been carried through in historical fact, the advance has usually been made amid the clash of opposing interests, so that compensation has not been given, and economic progress has accumulated a roll of victims, sufficient to give all sound policy a bad name (ibid.).

In its alternative interpretation, that is, requiring actual compensation, the Kaldor–Hicks test has drawn criticism, the principal objection being that, if applied to every single policy measure "compensation payments are not feasible politically" (Scitovsky 1951: 307, Chapter 7 in this volume).[69] The transaction costs of working out in every single instance a compensation scheme that has a chance of being generally accepted[70] would, quite obviously, be prohibitively high, in particular because of the problems created by the strategic bargaining it would invite.

The Kaldor–Hicks criterion was meant to achieve both, to account for the Robbins-critique of the "old," utilitarian welfare economics and to overcome the limitations of the Pareto criterion. Closer examination leads one, though, to conclude that it accomplishes neither. In its interpretation as a hypothetical compensation test it in effect falls back on the utilitarian concept of balancing satisfaction between persons;[71] if interpreted as requiring factual compensation it amounts to no more than the Pareto criterion it is supposed to supersede.[72] This is the conclusion Amartya Sen (1987: 386) draws when he notes:

> There had been earlier attempts to by-pass the need for utility comparisons by using the notion of compensation tests … However, the relevance of the compensation tests suffers from the following limitation. If compensations are not paid, then it is not clear in what way the situation can be taken to be an improvement (since those who have lost may be a great deal poorer, needier or more deserving – whatever our criteria for such judgment might be – than the gainers). And if compensations *are* in fact paid, then *after* the compensation what we observe is a Pareto improvement, so that no compensation tests are in fact needed. Thus, the compensation approach suffers from having to face the choice between being unconvincing or being irrelevant.

Hicks (1939: 712, Chapter 5 in this volume) had closed his 1939 article with the claim:

> I have accomplished my end if I have demonstrated the right of Welfare Economics – the "Utilitarian Calculus" of Edgeworth – to be considered an integral part of economic theory, capable of the same logical precision and the same significant elaboration as its twin brother, Positive Economics, the "Economic Calculus."

Yet, looking back at the history of efforts to develop the compensation approach into a firm foundation for welfare economics, critics have passed a more negative judgment.

> [J]udged in relation to its basic objective of enabling economists to make welfare prescriptions without having to make value judgments and, in particular, interpersonal comparisons of utility, the New Welfare Economics must be considered a failure (Chipman and Moore 1978: 548).[73]

> The "old" welfare economics of Pigou failed to elicit general support from economists because of its unwarranted – "unscientific" – informational basis, which is utilitarian in nature. The "new" welfare economics, which endeavored to do without cardinality and interpersonal comparability of welfare, also failed to provide a consistent analytical framework. … It seems to us that the widely held apathy and cynicism towards welfare economics in general and the "new" welfare economics in particular, have much to do with the Sisyphean labor expended by the compensation school of thought (Suzumura 2000: 6).

3.2.2 THE BERGSON–SAMUELSON SOCIAL WELFARE FUNCTION

Speaking of the compensation school as the "narrow version" of the New Welfare Economics, Paul Samuelson credits Abram Bergson's 1938 article "A Reformulation of Certain Aspects of Welfare Economics" with pioneering the, in his judgment, superior alternative version which has come to be known as the *Bergson–Samuelson social welfare function*.[74] In his paper, which he wrote as a Harvard graduate student,[75] and in the first footnote of which he thanks his fellow student "Mr. Paul Samuelson for suggestions on many points" (Bergson 1938: 310),[76] Bergson argued that "for the derivation of the conditions of maximum economic welfare" (Bergson 1938: 310) the Pareto criterion as a necessary but not sufficient requirement must be supplemented by some explicit value judgment specified as a social welfare function that allows for a selection among Pareto optima[77] or, in other words, for deciding on distributional issues.[78] It can be read as a summary of Bergson's principal tenets when Oscar Lange (1942: 223) states:

> The propositions of welfare economics can be divided into two parts. One part is … concerned with conditions which permit increasing the utility of one individual without diminishing the utility of anybody else. It comprises all propositions of welfare economics except those which relate to the optimum distribution of incomes. … The other part requires the setting up of a social value function W (u) which is maximized.[79]

According to Samuelson (1981: 225), who always stressed Bergson's primacy,[80] "it took more than a decade after 1938 for the Bergsonian message to be understood," and it was, in fact, the "Welfare Economics" chapter in Samuelson's most influential *Foundations of Economic Analysis* that secured the Bergson–Samuelson welfare function approach the dominant place it was able to occupy for many decades in modern welfare economics.[81]

Like the compensation school, the Bergson–Samuelson social welfare function takes its departure from "the evaluations of the individual members of the community" (Bergson 1938: 327), and it remains, in this sense, within the normative individualistic framework of the welfarist tradition. Yet, while it is often described as "an individualistic social welfare function:

one that 'respects' individual valuations" (Hands 2013: 5), it is "individualistic" only in a qualified sense, being subject to what Arrow (1969: 223, Chapter 20 in this volume) has called a "second order evaluation," a "second level at which the individual judgments are themselves evaluated."[82] As Samuelson has put it:

> Bergson defined and clarified the concept of an individualistic social welfare function – which ethically orders the various states of the world and which lets "individual tastes 'count,' in the sense of agreeing with individuals' orderings when those orderings are unanimous and resolving them ethically when they are not unanimous (Samuelson 1981: 224).[83]

While it is the task of the Bergson–Samuelson social welfare function to perform the "second-order evaluation," it is, according to Samuelson (1954: 387), "not a 'scientific' task of the economist to 'deduce' the form of this function," or, in other words, to determine on which ethical criterion it should be based. It can, he argues, "have as many forms as there are possible ethical views" (ibid.), and the only restriction based on it "is that it shall always increase or decrease when any one person's ordinal preference increases or decreases, all others staying on their same indifference level" (ibid.). In fact, as far as his own attitude in this matter is concerned, Samuelson expresses total indifference:

> Without inquiring into its origins, we take as a starting point of our discussion a function … which is supposed to characterize some ethical belief – that of a benevolent despot, or a complete egoist, or "all men of good will," a misanthrope, the state, race, or group mind, God, etc. …. We only require that the belief be such as to admit of an unequivocal answer as to whether one configuration of the economic system is "better" or "worse" than any other or "indifferent," and that those relationships are transitive (Samuelson 1947: 221, Chapter 6 in this volume).[84]

In his pioneering article Bergson had equally, though in less brash and more moderate terms, noted that the social welfare function approach is, per se, entirely neutral in regard to the ethical principle it is supposed to reflect. As he put it:

> In general, any set of value propositions which is sufficient for the evaluation of all alternatives may be introduced, and for each of these sets of propositions there corresponds a maximum position. The number of sets is infinite (Bergson 1938: 323).[85]

Yet, Bergson lets the quoted statement be followed immediately by a qualification concerning the "infinite number of sets":

> [I]n any particular case the selection of one of them must be determined by its compatibility with the value prevailing in the community the welfare of which is being studied. For only if the welfare principles are based on prevailing values can they be relevant to the activity of the community in question. But the determination of prevailing values for a given community, while I regard it as both a proper and necessary task for the economist … is a project which I shall not undertake here (Bergson 1938: 323)

Bergson's qualification of the ethical neutrality of the social welfare function serves as a reminder of the fact, discussed earlier, that welfare economics as an applied science advances hypothetical imperatives that can be expected to find an interested audience only among addressees who share the value judgment, or the normative criterion, upon which welfare economists base their analysis.[86] Samuelson is surely right when he posits that it "is a legitimate exercise of economic analysis to examine the consequences of various value judgments, whether or not they are shared by the theorist" (1947: 220, Chapter 6 in this volume). Yet, if they want to contribute to solving real world problems that people outside of academia care about, rather than only playing intellectual games within their academic peer group, welfare economists can scarcely afford the detached attitude Samuelson (1981: 228) displays when he proclaims:

> In my writing on the subject ... I have not shown much interest in the process by which particular social welfare functions arise and are deemed to be of interest or relevance. I have been satisfied to consider it not to be the task of economics as such to pass judgment on whether this social welfare function is in some sense more important than that social welfare function.

Of particular interest in the context of the present study is, though, a more fundamental question: what does the Bergson–Samuelson approach contribute to answering the research problem that, as I have argued above, has traditionally been the central concern of political economy, namely to explore what can be said about policy issues *if* the valuations of the individuals concerned are taken as the relevant normative standard or, in other words, if the premise of normative individualism is accepted? When Samuelson notes as a distinguishing mark of Bergson's social welfare function, by contrast to the "narrow version" of the New Welfare Economics, that it introduces an ethical norm "from outside positive economic science" (Samuelson 1981: 225), he implies an ambiguous claim. This could be read as the claim that, in Arrow's terminology, only the "second-order evaluation" of the social welfare function is introduced from outside positive economics, while the Paretian "first-order evaluation" in terms of individuals' own judgment can be viewed as part of positive economic science. The normative individualism presumed by the Pareto judgment is, however, clearly itself a value judgment that cannot be deduced from positive economic statements, a fact that Samuelson (1958: 540) points to when, in commenting on the Paretian "necessary (but not sufficient) condition" for a social optimum, he notes:

> Pareto, for reasons that I have never found convincing, tried to elevate these *necessary* conditions for an optimum into a *wertfrei* system of "new welfare economics" (ibid.)

The "first-order evaluation" beyond which the Bergson–Samuelson approach is said to move, can be described as "inside economics" only in the sense that it reflects the normative individualism that has traditionally been the starting premise of political economy as an applied science, a political economy that submits to the constraint of judging policy measures exclusively in terms of individuals' own evaluations. The old as well as the new welfare economics can be seen as part of an unfolding research tradition seeking to answer this challenge. By introducing a social welfare function as a "second-order evaluation," as a normative standard that is independent of, and can overrule, the evaluations of the individuals concerned, the Bergson– Samuelson approach simply abandons the defining constraint of the individualist research tradition. It does not "surpass" the "narrow" version of the new welfare economics in terms of the traditional research agenda, but rather changes the "rules of the game."

On "the explicit resort to external and nonindividualistic criteria" that the "social welfare function" approach implies, Buchanan ([1968] 1999: 183f.) comments:

> The basic inconsistency between this and the whole Paretian edifice was either not appreciated or deliberately ignored. … If external criteria are introduced to resolve distributional issues … why should norms based exclusively on individual preference orderings be honored.

3.3 Harsanyi's Utilitarian Equiprobability Model

In response to the critique of the "old" welfare economics, the "new" welfare economics abandoned the utilitarian project of assessing social welfare in terms of cardinally measured individual utilities. In contrast, John Harsanyi (1977b: 64)[87] explicitly advocates a concept of "social welfare or social utility" that, as he emphasizes, "clearly belongs to the utilitarian tradition."[88] In retrospect he comments:

> Utilitarian theory assumes that different people's utilities are cardinal quantities measurable on an interval scale and admit of meaningful interpersonal comparison. It *has* to make these assumptions because it makes maximization of expected social utility the basic criterion of morality, defining social utility as the arithmetic mean (or possibly as the sum) of individual utilities. Yet, this definition (in either form) will make sense only if individual utilities are cardinally measurable and are interpersonally comparable. … (Note that many economists would employ the term "social welfare function" to describe what I am calling "social utility" or "social utility function".)
>
> A generation ago, most economists and philosophers utterly rejected cardinal utility as well as interpersonal comparability. My own defense of these notions at the time (Harsanyi 1953 and 1955) was unmistakably a rather rare minority view (1988: 127, Chapter 14 in this volume).

Claiming that "philosophers and economists influenced by logical positivism have greatly exaggerated the difficulties in making interpersonal utility comparisons" (ibid.: 132), Harsanyi insists that

> the practical need for reaching decisions on public policy will require us to formulate social welfare functions – explicitly or implicitly – even if we lack the factual knowledge needed for placing interpersonal comparisons of utility on an objective basis (1969: 60).[89]

And he posits:

> Therefore, given enough information about the relevant individuals' psychological, biological, social, and cultural characteristics, as well as about the general psychological laws governing human behavior, *inter*personal utility comparisons in principle should be no more problematic than *intra*personal utility comparisons are between the utilities that the *same* person would derive from various alternatives under different conditions (1977b: 59).[90]

In his own approach to the subject, Harsanyi (1969: 55) notes, "*welfare economics* becomes a subdivision of ethics," conceived as "a theory of rational behavior in the service of the common interests of society as a whole" ([1977] 1982: 43).[91] As a subdivision of ethics, welfare economics in Harsanyi's account is based on a "model for moral value judgments" ([1977] 1982: 44), a model for how to rank "alternative social situations from a moral (or social) point of view" (1977b: 50). And to judge from a moral point of view, so he specifies, means to judge in terms of "impartial and impersonal criteria" rather than one's "own personal preferences and personal interests" (ibid.: 49).[92] Because in judging impartially a person "will by definition always assign the same weight to all individuals' interests, including his own" ([1977] 1982: 47), Harsanyi concludes that a *rational* impartial individual will rank social situations "according to the *arithmetic mean* of the utility levels that the individual members of society would enjoy in this situation" (1977b: 49), and that moral judgments are about maximizing this arithmetic mean.[93]

The requirements of impartiality and rationality can, Harsanyi argues, be more precisely described by what he calls the *equiprobability model*, a decision model based on the assumption of – to borrow Rawls' phrase – a choice behind a *veil of ignorance*.[94]

> To make it more precise, let us assume that he would choose between the two systems under the assumption that, in either system, he would have the same probability of occupying any one of the available social positions. In this case, we could be sure that his choice would be independent of morally irrelevant selfish considerations. Therefore his choice (or his judgment of preference) between the two systems would now become a genuine moral value judgment. ... For short reference, the fictitious assumption of having the same probability of occupying any possible social position will be called the equiprobability postulate, whereas the entire preceding decision model based on this assumption will be called the equiprobability model of moral value judgments ([1977] 1982: 45).[95]

Formally the equiprobability model can be interpreted as a model of "choice among alternative *risky projects*" (1977b: 50), according to which an individual's "choice would be rational only if it maximized his *expected utility*" (ibid.),[96] a calculation for which, Harsanyi (1988: 127, Chapter 14 in this volume) notes, "to use von Neumann-Morgenstern (vNM) utility functions" is an "obvious possibility."[97] The same reasoning that according to the equiprobability model applies to any individual as a member of the society in question would also apply, Harsanyi ([1977] 1982: 46) argues, "if he were an interested outsider rather than a member." As he explains:

> Indeed, for some purposes it is often heuristically preferable to restate the model under this alternative assumption. Yet, once we do this, our model becomes a modern restatement of Adam Smith's theory of an impartially sympathetic observer (ibid.).

Harsanyi acknowledges that "in the real world" value judgments concerning social welfare are usually not made from behind a veil of ignorance.[98] Yet, he posits:

> Of course, it is not really necessary that a person who wants to make a moral judgment ... should be literally ignorant of the actual social position that he does occupy or would occupy under each

system. But it *is* necessary that he should at least try his best to disregard this morally irrelevant piece of information when he is making his moral assessment. Otherwise his assessment will not be a genuine moral value judgment but rather will be merely a judgment of personal preference ([1977]: 1982: 45).

At the beginning of this section I quoted Harsanyi's claim that his approach to welfare economics "clearly belongs to the utilitarian tradition." And a statement like the following sounds very much like ordinary utilitarianism:

> The utilitarian theory I have proposed defines social utility in terms of individual utilities, and defines each person's utility function in terms of his personal preferences. Thus, in the end, social utility is defined in terms of people's preferences. This approach may be called preference utilitarianism ([1977] 1982: 54).[99]

Yet, it should be apparent by now that Harsanyi's approach is, as he explicitly acknowledges, a "qualified form of utilitarianism" (1977b: 64). In his "qualified utilitarianism" individuals' preferences are not unconditionally respected but are respected only if they are "worthy to be respected." As Harsanyi states:

> In my opinion social utility must be defined in terms of people's true preferences rather than in terms of their manifest preferences ([1977] 1982: 55).

There is an obvious tension in Harsanyi's approach. On the one hand it is, like ordinary preference utilitarianism, supposed to be based on an "individualistic ethic" that "requires the use ... of individual utilities not subject to restrictive postulates,"[100] and a commitment to the "principle of *preference autonomy*," according to which "in deciding what is good and what is bad for a given individual, the ultimate criterion can only be his own wants and his own preferences" ([1977] 1982: 55),[101] or to the "*principle of acceptance*" that "requires us to accept each individual's own personal preference as the basic criterion for assessing the utility (personal welfare) that he will derive from any given situation" (1977b: 52). On the other hand, the individual utilities or personal preferences which, according to Harsanyi, deserve to be respected in determining social utility are not, as is the case in ordinary utilitarianism, the utilities or preferences as seen by the individuals themselves but rather utilities and preferences that survive what commentators have described as a process of "laundering" or "purification."[102] As Harsanyi explains:

> Any sensible ethical theory must make a distinction between rational wants and irrational wants, or between rational preferences and irrational preferences. ... In actual fact, there is no difficulty in maintaining this distinction even without an appeal to any other standard than an individual's own personal preferences. All we have to do is to distinguish between a person's manifest preferences and his true preferences. His manifest preferences are his actual preferences as manifested in his observed behavior, including preferences possibly based on erroneous factual beliefs, or on careless logical analysis, or on strong emotions that at the moment greatly hinder rational choice. In contrast, a person's true preferences are the preferences he *would* have if he had all the relevant factual information, always reasoned with the greatest possible care, and were in a state of mind most conducive to rational choice ([1977]: 1982: 55f.).[103]

Responding to the critique leveled against the "old" welfare economics' method of assessing social welfare, the "new" welfare economics sought to come up with novel solutions avoiding the disputed assumptions of measurability and interpersonal comparability of utilities, only to be plagued by deficiencies of its own. Rejecting the critique of the utilitarian assumptions as exaggerated, Harsanyi claims to offer with his equiprobability approach a solution that "clearly belongs to the *utilitarian* tradition." Yet, on closer examination his "solution" turns out not to offer an answer to the challenge that the welfarist tradition struggled with, namely to derive a measure of social welfare from individuals' own evaluations, but, instead, to redefine the problem that is to be solved. Instead of answering this challenge, Harsanyi answers the *different* question of how a measure of social welfare can be determined if we start from what individuals' evaluations are after they have been purged from inappropriate or undeserving preferences.

As I have argued above, rather than classifying welfare economics as *"normative"* economics, it should more appropriately be understood as an *applied* economics, pronouncing *hypothetical imperatives* that inform interested addressees about suitable means for achieving hypothesized aims. Specifically, based on the premise of a normative individualism, welfare economics in this sense seeks to advance conjectures about the suitability of policy measures if the evaluations of the individuals concerned are taken as the relevant normative standard. It is significant that Harsanyi speaks of *hypothetical imperatives* in describing his own theory, and it is worth taking a closer look at his respective arguments.

When he characterizes his approach as "qualified" utilitarianism, Harsanyi does not only want to emphasize, as reported above, that it accepts individuals' utility functions not uncritically but only with appropriate corrections.[104] He also stresses that it "represents rule utilitarianism, not act utilitarianism" (1977b: 64). His position, as he puts it, "represents a doubly qualified form of utilitarianism" (ibid.). In his, as he calls it, *"critical rule utilitarianism,"*[105] social utility is meant to serve "primarily as a criterion to judge alternative moral rules and indeed alternative institutional arrangements for society" (ibid.). Accordingly, Harsanyi's approach to welfare economics may be said to have its primary focus on social rules and institutions, and one might expect that its primary purpose as applied economics is to provide guidance for the choice of rules and institutions, that is, to pronounce hypothetical imperatives for prudent rules choice.[106]

As has been argued above, hypothetical imperatives must be directed at addressees to whose supposed interests they appeal, showing that, given these interests, it is prudent for them to heed the advice. Harsanyi's "qualified" utilitarianism defines social utility, the criterion for evaluating rules and institutions, in terms of individuals' moral preferences, that is, the preferences they would hold if they were to judge from a moral point of view, or from the perspective of an "intelligent and sympathetic observer" who will respect only people's "true preferences and true interests" (1988: 131, Chapter 14 in this volume), their "genuine preferences" (ibid.: 132) or their "legitimate interests" (1977b: 48) in defining social utility. Even though Harsanyi posits that such a qualification is meant to be "achieved without reference to any standard outside of the own attitudes of the persons concerned" (1958: 312),[107] his hypothetical imperatives are obviously not meant to appeal to the preferences as defined by the individuals themselves, but to the preferences they would have after having been purified from those elements that an "informed and sympathetic observer" deems illegitimate. In other words, Harsanyi's hypothetical imperatives are not meant to show what is prudent to choose in terms of the addressees' own self-defined preferences, but rather what prudence would require if they would act on their "true" and "legitimate" preferences.

In section 5 below I shall discuss a different outlook on the issue of rule choice or *constitutional* choice, namely the research program of *constitutional political economy* which answers the problem that Harsanyi seeks to address by invoking people's *hypothetical moral preferences* in a more straightforward manner. This research program's hypothetical imperatives appeal to individuals' *actual, self-defined constitutional preferences*, that is, their preferences regarding the kind of rule regime or institutional framework under which they would want to live. In some of his comments on the nature of moral rules, Harsanyi does in fact invoke such an alternative perspective, and it is instructive to take a closer look at his arguments.

Moral rules and "their nearest relatives," such as "rules of a game, rules of etiquette, or legal rules," Harsanyi (1958: 308) argues, are "hypothetical imperatives of the noncausal type" in the sense that they "do not tell us what to do in order to produce certain particular results, but rather tell us what to do to make our behavior (and the consequences of our behavior) satisfy certain formal criteria" (ibid.). They serve, he states, "as possible reasons (i.e. rational motives) for a person to perform the acts enjoined by these rules" (ibid.: 307) as rational motives in the sense that "they are advices for people who already have a certain moral attitude, telling them what sort of behavior is consistent with the moral attitude they entertain" (ibid.: 308).[108] And he argues further:

> [T]he immediate reason for which people are morally bound to do certain acts is not social expedience: it is rather the existence of these obligations themselves, and possibly the existence of corresponding rights on the part of other people. But the existence itself of these obligations and rights, on the other hand, has to be explained in terms of the social expediency of this system of obligations and rights (ibid.: 313).

It helps to clarify matters if one explicitly distinguishes three issues concerning the "rationality of morality" that Harsanyi refers to in his comments. These are

- firstly, the question of what may be rational reasons for individuals to act in particular instances according to certain moral rules;
- secondly, the question of what may be rational reasons for individuals to adopt an attitude or general disposition to follow such rules; and,
- thirdly, the question of what may be rational reasons for individuals to wish that such rules be respected in the society in which they live.

With regard to the first issue, Harsanyi argues, coming close to a tautology, that moral rules provide such immediate reasons for individuals who have already adopted a disposition to follow them. The second issue he does not address directly, but indirectly he hints at the direction in which an answer may be sought. Noting the difficulties "ordinary utilitarianism" faces in accounting for the fact that "common sense regards moral obligations as binding even if in particular cases fulfillment of these obligations has predominantly bad consequences (with the possible exception of extreme cases)" (1958: 313), he argues that these difficulties can be overcome if the utilitarian criterion is applied not to the consequences of each *single* act but rather to the cumulative consequences of the general practice of acting in a certain particular way (acting according to a certain rule) in all similar cases (ibid.).

In so arguing Harsanyi does in effect make a case for the claim that it may well be rational for individuals, in terms of their ordinary preferences, to adopt a generalized moral disposition if the "cumulative consequences" of acting on such a disposition are superior to the outcome pattern that would result if they were to decide in each instance whether or not to follow the rule in question, given the particular circumstances of the case.[109] Circumstances that are conducive for moral dispositions to be rational in this sense are, obviously, likely to exist in societies or groups in which the respective moral rules are effectively, either formally or informally, enforced – which leads to the third question of why individuals may wish this to be the case in the society or group to which they belong.

In Harsanyi's approach the third issue is about *social* utility, defined in terms of individuals' *moral* preferences. Accordingly, in his account, their *moral* preferences, that is, the preferences they would have if they were to judge matters from a "moral point of view," must be supposed to provide the rational motives for individuals who want the rules in question to prevail in their community. Again, Harsanyi hints at a more straightforward explanation in terms of individuals' *factual* preferences when he argues:

> [A]n intelligent and sympathetic observer will obviously take into account not only the consequences of particular acts but also the cumulative long-run consequences of the general observance of the moral rules he recommends (and the cumulative long-run consequences of the system of obligations and rights established by these rules) (1958: 314).

Members of a group facing the need to choose the rules under which they are to live will surely consider the long-run cumulative consequences or, in other words, the general working properties, of potential alternative rules. Given sufficient uncertainty about how they themselves will be affected, their rule preferences or constitutional preferences may well serve as rational motives for them to agree on rules that they all expect to benefit from. As will be discussed in more detail below (section 5), it is from such a perspective, that is, by distinguishing between individuals' preferences over *actions* and their factual *constitutional* preferences, that the research program of constitutional political economy approaches the problem that Harsanyi sought to illuminate by contrasting individuals' "manifest" and their "moral" preferences.

4   The Preference-Individualism of Social Choice Theory

Kenneth Arrow's *Social Choice and Individual Values* ([1951] 1963)[110] is generally credited with having given birth to modern social choice theory, a research program that reactivates an earlier theoretical tradition associated with the French mathematicians Jean-Charles Borda (1781) and Jean-Antoine Condorcet (1785).[111] Next to Arrow, Amartya Sen is presumably the most prominent among the advocates of this research program. This chapter deals with the perspectives from which these two major representatives of the field approach their subject.

4.1   Kenneth Arrow's "Impossibility Theorem"

Like his 18th century predecessors, Arrow was interested in the problem of collective decisions and the inconsistencies they may involve.[112] Arrow's work is best known for his "impossibility theorem," showing that such inconsistencies arise not only with majority rule, as had been demonstrated by the early social choice theorists, but are more generally a problem that plagues group decisions.[113]

According to Arrow, the problem social choice theory deals with "is the aggregation of the multiplicity of individual preference scales about alternative social action" (1969: 223, Chapter 20 in this volume), and its purpose is "to analyze policy decisions" with the intention "to provide a rational framework for decisions that, for whatever reason, have to be made collectively" (1997: 3).[114] When he speaks of social choice theory's concern with "the justification of economic policy" (1987: 124),[115] Arrow explicitly adopts the premise of normative individualism as providing the criterion in terms of which legitimacy is to be judged.[116] As he puts it:

> The individual plays a central role in social choice as the judge of alternative social actions according to his own standards. We presume that each individual has some way of ranking social actions according to his preferences for their consequences (1969: 221, Chapter 20 in this volume).[117]

Apparently concerned about how the task of judging policy decisions according to a normative standard can be a legitimate part of positive economics,[118] Arrow refers to Hume's argument on the gulf between "is" and "ought" statements, adding:

> Obviously, in some sense, this must be right, but the examination of social choice theory suggests that the dichotomy is more blurred than it seems (2010: 25).

Counter to Arrow's concerns, there is no reason, though, to blur Hume's dichotomy if one interprets social choice theory, in the sense discussed above, as an *applied* economics that explores what can be said about policy issues *if* individuals' preference orderings are to serve as the criterion of evaluation.

Expressly regarding his approach as a contribution to the social welfare function discussion, Arrow notes in reference to Bergson's seminal article:

> [E]ssentially he is describing the process of assigning a numerical social utility to each social state, the aim of society then being described by saying that it seeks to maximize the social utility or social welfare subject to whatever technological or resource constraints are relevant or, put otherwise, that it chooses the social state yielding the highest possible social welfare within the environment ([1951] 1963: 22).

Different from Bergson's social welfare function which is about how measures of individual utility or welfare can be aggregated into some compound measure of *social welfare*, Arrow's approach is concerned with the aggregation of individuals' preference orderings into a *social preference ordering*.[119] As he puts it:

[L]et R_i be the ordering relation for alternative social states from the standpoint of individual i. ... Similarly, society as a whole will be considered provisionally to have a social ordering relation for alternative social states, which will be designated R. ... Throughout this analysis it will be assumed that individuals are rational ... The problem will be to construct an ordering relation for society as a whole that will also reflect rational choice-making ([1951] 1963: 19).[120]

In deriving a social preference ordering from individual orderings, Arrow applies the concept of rationality – characterized by consistency and transitivity in the preferences between different pairs of alternatives ([1951] 1963: 13) – equally to individual as well as to social choices.[121]

In analogy with the usual utility analysis of the individual consumer ..., rational behavior on the part of the community would mean that the community order the ... alternatives according to its collective preferences once and for all and then chooses in any given case that alternative among those actually available which stands highest on this list ([1951] 1963: 2).[122]

As noted before, Arrow sees his inquiry into *rational social choice* as a contribution to the project of welfare economics. If one identifies, as he does, "rationality with maximization," then, so he argues, "the problem of achieving a social maximum derived from individual desires is precisely the problem which has been central to the field of welfare economics" ([1951] 1963: 3). Accordingly, he defines the procedure for deriving a social ordering from individual orderings as a *social welfare function*:

By a social welfare function will be meant a process or rule which, for each set of individual orderings R_1, ..., R_n for alternative social states (one ordering for each individual), states a corresponding social ordering of alternative social states, R (ibid.: 22).

Whether such an aggregation exercise should indeed be called a social welfare function and, accordingly, be considered a contribution to welfare economics, has been the subject of considerable controversy. Very much at the center of this controversy is the issue of what the core piece of Arrow's work, the so-called impossibility theorem, implies for the welfare economics project.

It is in particular because of what he called "The General Possibility Theorem" ([1951] 1963: 46ff.), and what is generally referred to as the *impossibility theorem*, that Arrow's approach became the founding contribution to social choice theory.[123] In retrospect Arrow has summarized the essence of this theorem as showing that four "reasonable sounding requirements" for social choice – namely "the condition of Collective Rationality," "the Pareto principle," the condition of "Non-Dictatorship," and the "Independence of Irrelevant Alternatives" – "are contradictory," meaning that there exists no method of aggregating individual preference orderings into a social ordering that simultaneously satisfies all four requirements (1974b: 270).[124]

In his first contribution on the subject, Arrow (1950, Chapter 17 in this volume) noted that his purpose is to show that the difficulties of aggregating individual preferences pointed out by previous authors, such as the paradox of voting, arise generally:

For any method of deriving social choices by aggregating individual preference patterns which satisfies certain natural conditions, it is possible to find individual preference patterns which give rise to a social choice pattern which is not a linear ordering (1950: 330, Chapter 17 in this volume).[125]

As noted, the question of whether Arrow's contribution is of relevance to welfare economics and, in particular, whether his theorem implies that, as he claims, it is "impossible to construct a social welfare function" (1950: 336, Chapter 17 in this volume), has been the subject of controversy (Pollack 1979: 73, 86; Suzumura 2004: 13, fn. 4). In an early comment, Ian Little (1952: 427, Chapter 18 in this volume) had censured Arrow for failing to draw "an important distinction" by calling "his function a social welfare function and a decision-making process." Little (ibid.: 432) concluded that, because it is in fact about the latter, "Arrow's work has no relevance to the traditional theory of welfare economics, which culminates in the Bergson–Samuelson formulation." It was in particular Samuelson who persistently charged Arrow with misusing the label "social welfare function" for his preference-aggregation rule,[126] noting for example:

I shall argue again here the thesis that the Arrow result is much more a contribution to the infant discipline of mathematical politics than to the traditional mathematical theory of welfare economics. I export Arrow from economics to politics because I do not believe that he has proved the impossibility of the traditional Bergson welfare function of economics, even though many of his less expert readers seem inevitably drawn into thinking so (Samuelson 1967: 42).

According to Samuelson (1983: xxii), what Arrow has called a social welfare function he should have called instead a "Constitutional Voting Function" or "Constitutional Function."[127] As he notes in his "Foreword" to Graaff's *Theoretical Welfare Economics*:

What Arrow has proved ... is the impossibility of what I prefer to call "a political constitution function", which would be able to resolve *any* interpersonal differences brought to it while at the same time satisfying certain reasonable and desirable axioms. This Arrow result ... throws new light on age-old conundrums of democracy. But it does not detract, I believe, from the Bergson formulations nor from the lasting value of the present work (Samuelson 1968: vii–viii).

Bergson (1954: 240) has, like Samuelson, also stated that in his opinion "Arrow's theorem is unrelated to welfare economics." On Arrow's rule for aggregating individual orderings of social states into a corresponding social ordering, he commented:

Although Arrow conceives of his rule as representing a political process, he has also identified it with the criterion of social welfare, the "social welfare function," that is employed as a standard for normative appraisal in welfare economics. That identification too has been vigorously disputed, and more recently Arrow has acknowledged that this rule might better be referred to as a "constitution" than as a "social welfare function," but the difference between these two aspects has still been held to be "largely terminological" (Bergson 1976: 173).

As Bergson notes, responding to his critics Arrow had, indeed, decided to rename his aggregation rule, stating:

> It would perhaps have been better for me to use a different term from "social welfare function" for the process of determining a social ordering or choice function from individual orderings … I will therefore now use the term "constitution" … The difference, however, is largely terminological; to have a social welfare function in Bergson's sense, there must be a constitution (Arrow 1963: 104f.).

Yet, as the qualifying concluding sentence indicates, Arrow did not consider the issue to be of substantive relevance, and he insisted

> that any attempt to divide welfare economics … from the theory of social choice must be artificial. At the very least, welfare economics, no matter how defined, has something to do with the public adoption of economic policy, and it is hard to see how any study of the formation of social decisions can have "no relevance to" or "no bearing on" welfare economics (ibid.: 108).[128]

Nevertheless, he did restate his impossibility theorem in these terms:

> *There can be no constitution simultaneously satisfying the conditions of Collective Rationality, the Pareto Principle, the Independence of Irrelevant Alternatives, and Non-Dictatorship* (1969: 228, Chapter 20 in this volume).

By renaming his preference-aggregation rule a constitution, Arrow may have avoided the objections raised by Little, Samuelson and Bergson, yet he invited new objections. Social choice theory is concerned with democratic politics, and constitutions of democratic polities are commonly understood to specify, in one way or another, how decisions made on behalf of the polity derive their legitimacy from the *votes* of the ultimate sovereigns, the citizens, not from their *preferences* as assessed by some observer.[129] Arrow blurs this difference when he states that "the construction of a constitution" is about the "fundamental problem of public value formation" (1969: 225, Chapter 20 in this volume), that a constitution "assigns to any set of individual preference orderings a rule for making society's choices" (ibid.), and that "in a general sense all methods of social choice are of the type of voting" (ibid.: 227).

In one of his early papers, Robert Sugden (1978: 250) has criticized Arrow's use of the term "constitution" as being at odds with "the use of this word in everyday speech." If by "constitution" one means "a procedure by which decisions are taken *by* (and not just *for*) individuals in society," Sugden (ibid.: 252) argues, "social decision making must be formulated in terms of actions and not (at least not directly) in terms of preferences" (ibid.). Sugden concludes:

> If a constitution is to be interpreted as a description of a procedure by which social choices are taken by individuals, it must correspond in some way to the concept of a voting system (ibid.: 253).

The ambiguity in Arrow's use of the word "constitution" is, in fact, closely related to his ambiguous use of the term "social choice." The very first sentence of his *Social Choice and Individual Values* reads:

In a capitalist democracy there are essentially two methods by which social choices can be made, voting typically used to make "political" decisions, and the market mechanism, typically used to make economic decisions ([1951] 1963: 1).

And, further down he states:

The methods of voting and the market ... are methods of assimilating the tastes of many individuals in the making of social choices (ibid.: 2).

...

In the following discussion ... the distinction between voting and the market mechanism will be disregarded, both being regarded as special cases of the more general category of collective social choice (ibid.: 3).

While one may well seek to apply to both, the "social states" resulting from the "market mechanism" and from "voting," methods of "amalgamating" individual preferences, it is surely difficult to see in what sense both, markets and voting, can be subsumed under the "category of collective social choice." There is a categorical difference between the two. To be sure, market outcomes result from individual choices which may be said to reflect the choosers' preferences, and they may, in this sense, be said to represent an "amalgamation" of individual preferences. Yet, market outcomes are not chosen in any meaningful sense by anyone. They simply result as the combined effects of separate individual choices, choices that are only directed at individual purposes and are not meant as inputs into a process that serves to produce the overall outcome. By contrast, the explicit purpose of voting is to produce collective choices, and the only meaning of the individual choices, the votes, is to serve as inputs into the political process.[130]

That "the voting process is fundamentally different from the market" and that "the market does not belong in the category of collective choice at all" is, in fact, the objection Buchanan (1954: 114, Chapter 19 in this volume) has emphasized in his critique of Arrow, arguing:

The market exists as a means by which the social group is able to move from one social state to another as a result of a change in the environment without the necessity of making a collective choice. ...

The market does not establish the optimum social state in the sense that individuals, if called upon to vote politically (act collectively) for or against the market-determined state in opposition to a series of alternatives, would consistently choose it. This may or may not be an important conclusion, depending on the value judgment made concerning the appropriateness of majority approval as the criterion of optimum collective choice. But the essential point here is that the market does not call upon individuals to make a decision collectively at all (ibid.: 122).[131]

4.2 *Amartya Sen's "Broadening of the Informational Base"*

Amartya Sen describes the research program of social choice theory as follows:

If there is a central question that can be seen as the motivating issue that inspires social choice theory, it is this: how can it be possible to arrive at cogent aggregative judgments about the society (for example, about "social welfare," or "the public interest," or "aggregative poverty"), given the diversity of preferences, concerns, and predicaments of the different individuals *within* the society? How can we find any rational basis for making such aggregative judgments as "the society prefers this to that," or "the society should choose this over that," or "this is socially right" (Sen 1999: 349).[132]

Or, in brief:

The typical social-choice theoretic format is that of transforming a set (in fact, an *n*-tuple) of individual preference orderings into a social preference relation or a social choice function (1986: 214).[133]

Like Arrow with his "impossibility theorem," Sen has spurred an extended debate among social choice theorists with an impossibility theorem of his own, called "the impossibility of a Paretian liberal" (1970). The theorem posits that there is a conflict between individual liberty and the Pareto principle, the, as Sen notes, "cornerstone of welfare economics which insists that unanimous individual preference rankings must be reflected in social decisions" (1983: 5).[134] Specifically, the theorem says that there "is no social decision function that can simultaneously satisfy condition U, P, and L" (Sen 1970: 153), a "social decision function" being defined as a "collective choice rule," as "a functional relationship that specifies one and only one social preference relation R for any set of n individual orderings (one ordering for each individual)" (ibid.: 152).[135] The individual orderings are supposed to be "over the set X of all possible social states, each social state being a complete description of society including every individual's position in it" (ibid.).

The conditions U (Unrestricted Domain), P (Pareto Principle) and L (Liberalism) Sen defines as follows:

Condition U: Every logically possible set of individual preference orderings is included in the domain of the collective choice rule.
Condition P: If every individual prefers any alternative *x* to another alternative *y*, then society must prefer *x* to *y*.
Condition L: For each individual *i*, there is at least one pair of alternatives, say (*x, y*), such that if this individual prefers *x* to *y*, then society must prefer *x* to *y*, and if this individual prefers *y* to *x*, then society should prefer *y* to *x* (ibid.: 153).[136]

The original example Sen used to illustrate the theorem is the following. There are two individuals, a copy of *Lady Chatterley's Lover*, and three social states: individual 1 (a "prude") reads it (*x*); individual 2 (a "lewd") reads it (*y*); no one reads it (*z*). Individual 1 (the prude) ranks the alternatives in the order *z, x, y*; individual 2 (the lewd) in the order *x, y, z*. As Sen reasons, if the choice is between the *x* and *z*,

someone with liberal values may argue that it is person 1's preference that should count; since the prude would not like to read it, he should not be forced to. Thus the society should prefer *z* to *x* (ibid.: 155).

Likewise, if the choice is between *y* and *z*,

> liberal values require that person 2's preference should be decisive … Hence *y* should be judged socially better than *z*. Thus, in terms of liberal values, … the society should prefer *y* to *z*, and *z* to *x*. This discourse could end happily with the book being handed over to person 2 but for the fact that it is a Pareto inferior alternative, being worse than person 1 reading it in the view of both persons, i.e., *x* is Pareto superior to *y* (ibid.).

As to the "moral" to be drawn from the theorem, Sen concludes:

> It is that in a very basic sense liberal values conflict with the Pareto principle. If someone takes the Pareto principle seriously, as economists seem to do, then he has to face problems of consistency in cherishing liberal values, even very mild ones. Or, to look at it in another way, if someone does have certain liberal values, then he may have to eschew his adherence to Pareto optimality (ibid.: 157).

Due to the nature of social choice theory as "a subject in which formal and mathematical techniques have been very extensively used" (1999: 353),[137] much of the debate on Sen's – as well as on Arrow's – impossibility theorem has been in such formal and mathematical terms. There is no need in the present context to cover this part of the debate. Of interest here are those contributions that address the theoretical-conceptual foundations of Sen's argument, such as his use of the term "liberty." What, in this context, is at issue Sen points out when he states:

> Liberty has many different aspects, including two rather distinct features: (1) it can help us to achieve what we would choose to achieve in our respective private domains, for example, in personal life (this is its "opportunity aspect"), and (2) it can leave us directly in charge of choices over private domains, no matter what we may or may not achieve (this is its "process aspect"). In social choice theory, the formulation of liberty has been primarily concerned with the former, that is, the opportunity aspect (1999: 363).

As noted, Sen defines the "liberalism" condition in his theorem in terms of individual *preferences*, namely as demanding

> that for each person there is at least one pair of social states, say, *x* and *y*, such that his preference over that pair must be decisive for social judgment; i.e., if he prefers *x* to *y*, then *x* must be acknowledged to be socially better than y and correspondingly if he prefers *y* to *x* (1976: 218).

To respect individuals' liberty means in Sen's theoretical framework to respect their *preference orderings over social states*. It is his very use of the terms "liberty" and "liberalism" that critics have censured to be in contrast to the common use of these terms.[138] Authors like Robert Nozick,[139] Brian Barry and Robert Sugden have pointed out that liberalism is not about individuals' preferences over social states but "a doctrine about who has what rights to control what" (Barry 1986: 15), that "a liberal is one who is willing to concede to others the freedom to make choices for themselves even if these choices run counter to his own preferences"

(Sugden 1978: 258).[140]

Responding to such criticism, Sen (1986: 224) maintains that the "view of 'liberty as control' is fundamentally inadequate and this characterization of liberalism is correspondingly defective," and he posits:

> [T]here is some real advantage in viewing liberty in terms of evaluation of overall states of affairs, and not just related to the single issue of procedure, to wit, who is actually exercising control. The characterization of liberty in social choice theory is, thus, not without merit, ... Finally, incorporating liberty in the judgments of states of affairs also has the further advantage of being able to take a more informed view of liberty than the procedural control view – blind to the outcomes – can permit. ... The simpler social choice characterizations catch one aspect of liberty well (to wit: whether people are getting what they would have chosen if they had control), but miss another (to wit: who actually controlled the decision). But the view of liberty as control misses the former important aspect altogether even though it catches the latter (1986: 231f.).[141]

Yet, with the reasons he invokes to justify his use of the term, Sen answers the charge that what he calls "indirect liberty" (1983: 19)[142] is quite different from what the term "liberty" is commonly understood to mean, and that, if one applies the common meaning, the alleged conflict between liberal values and the Pareto principle disappears.[143]

To restate this charge in terms of the distinction that is of principal interest in the present context, namely between preference-individualism and choice-individualism: Sen treats as belonging to one normative dimension what in fact are two paradigmatically different principles, one requiring that individuals' *preferences over outcomes* (social states) are to be respected, the other requiring that individuals' *choices among actions* are to be respected.[144] It is, in effect, this distinction that the social choice theorists Gaertner, Pattanaik and Suzumura (1992) invoke in their "*game form approach* to individual rights" (Suzumura 1996: 28) that they present as an alternative to Sen's conceptualization. This is how they define this approach:

> Formally, a game form is a specification of:
> a set N of n players;
> a set S_k of strategies for each player $k \in N$;
> a set X of all feasible outcomes; and
> an outcome function which specifies exactly one outcome for each ... |N|-tuple of strategies, one strategy for each player.
> ... The content of individual rights in this framework lies in a specification of the admissible strategies for each player $k \in N$, and the complete freedom of each player to choose any of the admissible strategies and/or the obligation of the agents not to choose a non-admissible strategy (Gaertner, Pattanaik and Suzumura 1992: 173).[145]

When stated in game form, it is apparent that "liberty" is about the choice among strategies, that is, actions, while preference orderings are over outcomes (social states). It may well be that from the players' strategy choices outcomes result that are inferior, in both players' judgment, to an outcome that would have resulted if they had chosen differently – an observation prominently exemplified by the so-called prisoners' dilemma. But this is not a *paradox*. It is simply a result of the given choice setting, a result that may provide prudential reasons for the players jointly to seek to modify the choice setting, that is, the "rules of the game" under which they choose. What this means for Sen's impossibility theorem Suzumura (1996: 29) states thus:

> [T]he game form articulation of individual libertarian rights based on the intuitive concept of freedom of choice is not just an alternative approach to Sen's classical articulation of individual liberty. It is also meant to cast serious doubt on Sen's approach.

There is another part of Sen's contribution to social choice that has found considerable attention, a part that is of particular interest in the present context as it pertains directly to the viability of the preference-individualist paradigm. On the one hand Sen argues that this paradigm is central to social choice theory, and he stresses that, while Arrow's format may have "been modified and extended in several ways,"

> the fundamental role of individual preferences has tended to survive. Even now the discipline of social choice theory is, to a great extent, correctly describable as being about "social choice and individual values" (1997: 17, Chapter 22 in this volume).

On the other hand, he not only emphasizes that the "foundational feature of social choice theory," namely "taking individual preferences as the basis of social choice, ... has been subjected to much criticism" (ibid.: 15). In his own work he has also persistently advocated a social choice theory that frees itself from the "informational constraint" of a "welfarism" that requires taking individual preferences as *the* starting point for normative judgments on social matters.[146] As he reasons:

> [I]t is convenient to distinguish between "utility information" in the general sense (including information about preference rankings) and "nonutility information" regarding other features of states of affairs. ... In his original formulation of the problem of social choice, Kenneth Arrow was moved by the view, common in positivist philosophy that was then influential in welfare economics, that "interpersonal comparisons of utilities have no meaning" (Arrow 1951: 9). The utility information that is usable in this structure of social choice consists of n-tuples of individual preferences (or utility orderings) of the respective individuals – considered separately. This is a momentous informational exclusion, the removal of which can open up many constructive possibilities (2010: 35).

In Sen's view, trying "to make social welfare judgments *without* using any interpersonal comparison of utilities, and *without* using any nonutility information, is not a fruitful enterprise" (1985: 8),[147] because, as he posits, there "are plenty of 'social choice problems'" the analysis of which requires one "to go beyond looking only for the best reflection of given individual preferences, or the most acceptable procedure for choices based on those preferences" (1995: 17, Chapter 21 in this volume).[148] Accordingly, Sen seeks to advance a social choice theory that allows for both interpersonal comparisons and nonutility information.[149]

With regard to the issue of interpersonal comparisons, Sen (1999: 357) notes that the "foremost question to be addressed is this: interpersonal comparisons of what?" And his answer is:

> The principal issue is the choice of some accounting of individual advantage, which need not take
> the form of comparisons of mental states of happiness, and could instead focus on some other way
> of looking at individual well-being or freedom of substantive opportunities (seen in the perspective
> of a corresponding evaluative discipline) (ibid.: 358).

As Sen recognizes, the original dispute about the interpersonal comparability of utility was, of
course, about the comparability of *mental states*, an issue that had its place within the
subjectivist-individualist paradigm as the traditional trademark of economic theory and
political economy. In distancing himself from what he calls an "overconcentration on
comparisons of mental states" (1999: 365) and in focusing on other ways of "looking at
individual well-being," Sen does not simply suggest a modification within the received
theoretical framework but a change in its paradigmatic foundation. To claim that nonutility
measures of welfare such as "incomes or commodity bundles, or resources more generally"
(1999: 358) can be compared across persons means to replace the comparability issue as
traditionally understood by an issue that was never under dispute and that obviously finds a
trivial solution.

Sen's call for admitting interpersonal comparisons amounts in essence to nothing other than
his plea for "broadening the informational basis" of social choice theory[150] by relying on
objectively identifiable welfare-indicators.[151] On this procedure he comments:

> This procedure can be improved upon by taking note not only of the ownership of primary goods
> and resources, but also of interpersonal differences in converting them into the capability to live
> well. Indeed, I have tried to argue in favor of judging individual advantage in terms of the respective
> capabilities, which the person has, to live the way he or she has reason to value (1999: 358).

It is, indeed, the latter aspect, the focus on capabilities, that Sen's work has been particularly
identified with, an aspect on which Suzumura (2000: 12) comments:

> To escape from the subjectivist mistake of welfarist-consequentialism ... and to gear more directly
> with individual advantages *per se*, Sen ... proposed that we should focus on what he christened
> *functionings*. ... The *capability* of a person is defined as the set of functioning vectors from which
> the person is capable of choosing. Thus, Sen's concepts of functionings and capabilities provide us
> with a spectacle through which we can examine the performance of alternative economic systems
> from the viewpoint of individuals' opportunities to realize the life they value on deliberation.

As an argument in favor of his plea for a broadening of the informational basis of social choice
theory, Sen points to research issues that, as he posits, require such "informational enrichment":

> We do care about the size and distribution of the overall achievements; we have reason to want to
> reduce deprivation, poverty, and inequality; and all these call for interpersonal comparisons –
> either of utilities or of other indicators of individual advantages, such as real incomes, opportunities,
> primary goods, or capabilities (1995: 8, Chapter 21 in this volume).

Sen is surely right in claiming that abandoning the "informational constraint" of traditional welfarism allows him to make judgments on the research issues he lists that would be excluded if he were to stick to the premise that welfare judgments are to be based on the evaluations of the individuals involved themselves. But it also means, as noted above, that he abandons the "rules of the game" that defined, since its utilitarian origins, the research program of classical political economy and its offspring, welfare economics and social choice theory. What Suzumura classifies as "subjectivist mistake" was an integral part of the *normative individualism* that was the, explicit or implicit, premise on which "welfarism" as an applied science based its hypothetical imperatives, namely that policies are to be judged in terms of how the individuals themselves judge their merits. A social choice theory as advocated by Sen that allows judgments on policy issues to be based not only on individual values but on "some other characteristics of the respective individuals,"[152] may well have its own merits, but it provides no longer answers to the problem that political economists, welfare economists and social choice theorists traditionally struggled with.

5 The Choice-Individualism of Constitutional Political Economy

Constitutional political economy, or *constitutional economics*, is a field of inquiry that has come to be known under its name only quite recently. The name was coined in the 1980s, as a dictionary entry it appeared first in 1987 (Buchanan [1987] 2001), and the journal *Constitutional Political Economy* was inaugurated in 1990.[153] Yet, the origins of the research program can be traced back to one of the first publications of its principal founder, James M. Buchanan. In his 1949 paper on "The Pure Theory of Government Finance" he challenged, as he put it in retrospect, "the still-dominant orthodoxy in public finance and welfare economics" (1987: 243, Chapter 38 in this volume)[154] by advocating an *individualistic* theory for which "the state has no ends other than those of its individual members" and state decisions are "the collective decisions of individuals" ([1949] 1999: 122f.).

5.1 The Normative Premise of Individual Sovereignty

Characteristic of the paradigm that Buchanan helped to create is its consistent individualism, both in its positive-explanatory (*methodological individualism*)[155] and in its normative-applied dimensions (*normative individualism*). Methodological individualism is commonly regarded as an attribute of economic theory in general,[156] but it is, as Buchanan charges, not always consistently adhered to, notably in public finance and in welfare economics, when it comes to accounting for *collective action*, the actions and decisions of organized collectivities or "corporate actors" (Vanberg 1992), in particular of "the state."[157]

When Buchanan describes his approach as an "individualistic theory of collective choice" (Buchanan and Tullock 1962: 2) or as a "purely individualistic conception of the collective" (ibid.: 13), this means specifically that individuals' choices – rather than individual *utilities* or *preferences* – are taken as the starting point for *explanation* as well as for the *evaluation* of collective phenomena. The explanatory task, Buchanan notes, requires that the political process "be 'factored down' to the level of individual choices" (1966: 27):

> Only individuals choose, only individuals act. An understanding of any social interaction process
> must be based on an analysis of the choice behavior of persons who participate in the process.
> Results that are predicted or that may be observed in social interaction must be factored down into
> the separate choices made by individuals (1989: 37f.).[158]

The principal focus of constitutional economics "in its positive aspects," as an *explanatory* enterprise, he describes as the "analysis of the working properties of ... alternative sets of rules and institutions that serve to constrain the choice behavior of participants" ([1989] 2001: 270).

Taking individuals' choices as a starting point for the evaluation of collective phenomena means to respect individuals as "ultimate sovereigns" ([1991] 1999: 288) in matters of collective choice. Accordingly, the "normative" task of constitutional economics as applied science is, in Buchanan's words,

> to assist individuals, as citizens, who ultimately control their own social order, in their continuing
> search for those rules of the political game that will best serve their purposes whatever these might
> be (1987: 250, Chapter 38 in this volume).

When he speaks of a "normative task," Buchanan leaves no doubt that this is not meant to claim for the constitutional political economist any authority to pronounce judgments on "what should be" as categorical imperatives.[159] It means that, in the sense discussed above, applying its positive findings to the solution of practical problems is seen as an essential task of political economy,[160] and that in taking on this task one must hypothesize some value judgment that defines the focus of inquiry, the criterion for what one considers the "problem" for which a solution is to be sought. And in Buchanan's case this value judgment is, as noted, a *normative individualism*, a premise that, in its general interpretation, he shares with the above-discussed research programs of welfare economics and social choice theory. Yet, as noted before, the way Buchanan specifies this premise is characteristically different from theirs. And the differences in the respective specifications of what a *normative individualism* entails have significant implications for how the three research programs – Buchanan's choice-individualism, welfare economics' utility-individualism and social choice theory's preference-individualism – define the problem for which they seek a solution and, accordingly, the foci of their inquiry. Or, stated in other words, in specifying what they mean by "normative individualism" differently, these research programs differ in their, as Buchanan calls it,[161] "self-imposed constraints."

In welfare economics, the premise of normative individualism is interpreted in the sense of "respecting individuals' tastes" (Samuelson 1977: 83), or as the postulate "that individuals' preferences are to 'count'" (Samuelson 1947: 223, Chapter 6 in this volume). Accordingly, the "self-imposed constraint" of this research program is to show how one can arrive at judgments on policy issues by starting from individuals' tastes or preferences and amalgamating them into some measure of aggregate welfare. Similarly, in social choice theory, the normative premise "that social choice depends on individual welfares" (Arrow 2010: 26) and "that *alternative policies should be judged on the basis of their consequences for individuals*" (Arrow 1987: 124) means that individuals' preferences are to be respected in the sense that "individual values are ... the raw material out of which the welfare judgment is manufactured"

(Arrow 1963: 104). And the problem to be solved concerns "the aggregation of the multiplicity of individual preference scales" (Arrow 1969: 223, Chapter 20 in this volume) into a social ordering.[162]

By contrast, in Buchanan's *choice-individualism* the premise of normative individualism means that individuals' choices are to be respected, that their choices are "the ultimate sources of evaluation" ([1985] 2001: 245). It means that the individuals composing a collective unit are viewed as "the ultimate sovereigns in matters of social organization" ([1991] 1999: 288), as "the ultimate decision-making authority" (Buchanan and Tullock 1962: 6) from whom any legitimacy to decide or act on behalf of the collective unit derives.[163] Accordingly, the problem to be solved is how collective decisions can be derived from individual choices and how, starting from individuals' choices, one can arrive at judgments on policy issues or social matters generally.[164]

Buchanan insists that for the purpose of judging policy issues

> the values or interests of individuals are the only values that matter for the quite simple reason that these are the only values that exist. Such terms as "national goals," "national interest," and "social objectives" are confusing at best ([1988] 2001a: 62).

And, taken seriously, the *subjectivism* which has traditionally been a core component of economists' outlook requires one to recognize that individuals' values or interests are not directly accessible for the observing economist but can only be inferred from actual choices. In supposing that the "observing economist is ... able to 'read' individual preference functions," Buchanan (1959: 126, Chapter 10 in this volume) charges, "welfare economists, new and old," have generally imputed an unfounded "omniscience in the observer" (ibid.).[165] In these constructions, he notes, "'utility' ... has a presumptive existence that is independent of any exercise of choice itself" ([1991] 1999: 282) and that "can, at least conceptually, be objectified and separated from individual choice" (ibid.: 283), constructions against which he objects:

> From a subjectivist perspective, a "utility function", as such, does not exist which, even conceptually, could be observed and recognized independently of an individual's choice behavior ([1991] 1999: 286.)[166]

Buchanan's choice-individualism with its above-described characteristics has two principal, interrelated implications for the research agenda that it informs. Firstly, if individuals' choices are taken as the criterion against which policy issues are to be judged, what may count as "socially desirable" cannot be determined in terms of presumed individual utilities or preferences but can only be inferred from *voluntary agreement* among the individuals concerned. As Buchanan puts it:

> If only individual evaluations are to count, and if the only source of information about such evaluations is the revealed choice behavior of individuals themselves, then no change can be assessed to be "efficient" until and unless some means could be worked out so as to bring all persons (and groups) into agreement ([1987] 2001: 10).

Secondly, if agreement is the relevant normative criterion, the focus of analysis must be on the process through which, and the rules and institutions under which, policy choices are made rather than on the resulting outcomes per se. Again, in Buchanan's words:

> That is "good" which "tends to emerge" from the free choices of the individuals who are involved. It is impossible for an external observer to lay down criteria for "goodness" independently of the process through which results or outcomes are attained. The evaluation is applied to the means of attaining outcomes, not to outcomes as such (1975: 6).

Buchanan ([1985] 2001: 249) refers to these two attributes when he speaks of his approach as a "contractarian-constitutionalist paradigm." The following sections 5.2–5.5 take a closer look at these two dimensions of Buchanan's approach to political economy, its *contractarianism* and its *constitutionalism*.

5.2 Contractarianism: The Unanimity Criterion

On several occasions, not least in his Nobel Prize lecture, Buchanan has acknowledged the intellectual debt he owes to Knut Wicksell's 1896 dissertation *Finanztheoretische Untersuchungen*, a book he by serendipity discovered and the central part of which, *Ueber ein neues Prinzip der gerechten Besteuerung*, he translated into English (Wicksell [1896] 1958, Chapter 24 in this volume).167 In "A New Principle of Just Taxation" Wicksell had argued that in a polity of free and equal citizens public expenditures can be considered legitimate only if they are "intended for an activity useful to the whole of society and so recognized by all" (ibid.: 89), since, so he argued, it "would seem to be a blatant injustice if someone should be forced to contribute toward the costs of some activity which does not further his interest" (ibid.).

He concluded that only unanimous approval of a proposed activity can be regarded as the ultimate test of whether it promises indeed net benefits for all members of the community. As he put it:

> In the final analysis, unanimity and fully voluntary consent in the making of decisions provide the only certain and palpable guarantee against injustice in tax distribution (ibid.: 90).

Due to the influence of Knut Wicksell on his own thinking, Buchanan reports,

> the rule of unanimity seemed to me to possess qualities that have largely been ignored. ... If we reject the notion that there must exist a public or general interest apart from that of the participants, we are necessarily led to the conclusion that only upon unanimous consent of all parties can we be absolutely assured that the total welfare of the group is improved. As applied to politics, the rule of unanimity is equivalent to the Paretian criterion for judging potential change to be optimal ([1968] 2000: 10).

The Wicksellian unanimity criterion takes in Buchanan's choice-individualist research program the place that in its utility- or preference-individualist counterpart the Pareto criterion occupies,[168] the latter requiring a "unanimity of preferences," the former a unanimity of actual choices as a test of "social efficiency."[169] About the preference-individualist version Sen notes:

The Pareto principle is sometimes referred to as the "unanimity rule"; requiring that preferences unanimously held must be fully reflected in social judgment (Sen 1976: 219f.).

Referring to the welfare economist's presumptive knowledge of individuals' utilities, Buchanan notes about the choice-individualist version:

> If the Paretian construction is translated into the Wicksellian framework, the economist escapes from the apparent necessity to know anything about individual preferences ([1988] 2001b: 139).[170]

The choice-individualist perspective of constitutional political economy suggests that two issues, the issue of *legitimacy* and the issue of *efficiency*, should be separated that are conflated in utility- or preference-individualist approaches. In the latter the proper aggregation of individuals' utilities or preferences identifies the "efficient," welfare maximizing policy measure and provides *thereby* "the justification of economic policy" (Arrow 1987: 124).[171] In choice- individualism agreement or unanimity plays two distinguishable roles, as *criterion of legitimacy* and as *test of efficiency*. According to "the normative premise of individuals as sovereigns" (Buchanan [1991] 1999: 288), voluntary agreement among the individuals involved is, on the one hand, considered the only source from which legitimacy in social matters can be derived, be it social transactions, collective choices, policies, or institutional arrangements.[172] On the other hand, from the choice-individualist perspective agreement among the parties involved provides the only conclusive test of efficiency in social matters, that is, of claims that transactions, policies, institutional reforms or other social changes are "welfare improving."[173] The difference between the roles of agreement as a criterion of legitimacy and as a test of efficiency has important implications for the role that *knowledge* on the part of the acting persons and of the observing economist plays in judging policy matters. As far as the legitimacy issue is concerned, Buchanan emphasizes:

> Individuals are to be allowed to choose among potentially available alternatives simply because they are the ultimate sovereigns. And this conclusion holds independently of the state of knowledge possessed about either means or ends ([1991] 1999: 288).

The normative premise of individual sovereignty does not place any knowledge requirements on individuals' authority to exercise their rights to choose, but requires that whatever they voluntarily agree upon be considered thereby legitimized.

By contrast, voluntary agreement among the parties involved does not require the observing economist to regard such agreement as the definitive judgment on whether the transactions or arrangements agreed upon are efficient in the sense that they actually turn out to produce welfare-enhancing results. The expectations of the parties involved concerning the welfare effects of what they agreed upon are necessarily based on conjectures about factual consequences, conjectures that may be mistaken.

Likewise, the political economists' claims about the welfare-enhancing qualities of policy measures can be no more than hypothetical judgments. They must be based on falsifiable conjectures about the results these measures will produce, and they must in addition be based on conjectures about the preferences the individuals involved hold in regard to these predicted results. While the former conjectures are to be tested against observable facts, the latter, being about subjective matters, can only be tested in terms of actual agreement among the respective individuals. As Buchanan states:

> The political economist is often conceived as being able to *recommend* policy A over policy B. If
> ... no objective social criterion exists, the economist *qua* economist is unable to recommend. ...
> But there does exist a positive role for the economist in the formation of policy. His task is that of
> diagnosing social situations and presenting to the choosing individuals a set of possible changes.
> ... The conceptual test is *consensus* among members of the choosing group, not objective
> improvement in some measurable social aggregate. ... Propositions of positive economics find
> their empirical support or refutation in observable economic quantities or in observable market
> behavior of individuals. Political economy differs in that its propositions find empirical support or
> refutation in the observable behavior of individuals *in their capacities as collective decision-
> makers* – in other words, in politics.
>
>   Propositions advanced by political economists must always be considered as tentative
> hypotheses offered as solutions to social problems. ... [The political economist] presents a possible
> change. But this change is a "cure" only if consensus is attained in its support (1959: 127f., Chapter
> 10 in this volume).

While the normative premise of individual sovereignty requires that individuals be respected as the *ultimate* judges on what furthers their interests, it does not entail the unqualified presumption, often associated with a normative individualism, that individuals "themselves know best what they want" (Little 1957: 258), or that the individual "is the best judge of his own well-being" (Mishan 1960: 199). As Buchanan notes:

> We may, for example, observe that persons sometimes regret choices that have been made, and we
> may conjecture that some third person might have been able to predict that such regret would
> occur, post choice. And we may then hypothesize that this third person might have been able to
> offer "good" advice to the chooser, pre choice ([1991] 1999: 287).

It is an obvious fact that individuals do make mistakes, that they do not "always know with certainty which of a set of alternative outcomes will make them better off *ex post facto*" (Buchanan [1968] 2000: 9), and that there are occasions when others would be better judges as to the welfare effects of their choices than the individuals themselves. Yet, all this does not alter the fact that, according to the choice-individualist approach, individuals' choices are to be respected as the ultimate source of legitimacy in social matters.[174]

The distinction between the role of agreement as criterion of legitimacy and as test of efficiency is of particular relevance for the study of policy choice in democratic society, where such choices are regularly made by less-than-unanimity, typically by majority rule. As will be discussed in more detail below (section 5.5), there are prudential reasons for members of polities to agree to a constitution that allows for sub-constitutional policy decisions to be made by less-than-unanimity rules. And it is their agreement to the constitution that confers legitimacy to the latter decisions; decisions that are themselves not supported by unanimous approval. These decisions can be said to be *indirectly* legitimized, deriving their legitimacy from the agreement to the procedure by which they are made.[175] Yet, since the sub-constitutional policy decisions are not unanimously approved, from a choice-individualist perspective definite judgments on their efficiency cannot be made. The political economist can pass judgment on their legitimacy, but must remain silent on their efficiency. As Buchanan notes:

> [A]ny departure from the strict unanimity requirement means that inefficient or nonoptimal outcomes may emerge. The final outcome of the collective decision process need not be Pareto optimal ([1967] 1999: 289).[176]

5.3 The Gains-From-Trade Paradigm

There exists, as Buchanan points out, a systematic connection between contractarianism and the exchange paradigm in economics: both assign a central role to voluntary agreement among the parties involved as the criterion of legitimacy and test of efficiency. When economists speak of markets as wealth-creating arrangements, they do not just mean any conceivable system of decentralized interactions but one framed by institutional provisions that aim at excluding force and fraud as instruments of enrichment and, thus, to ensure voluntariness in transactions. "The market" is, in Buchanan's (1964: 219, Chapter 26 in this volume) words, "the embodiment of the voluntary exchange processes that are entered into by individuals in their several capacities."[177] The economists' standard notion of the efficiency of the outcomes market transactions produce can, in this sense, find its ultimate basis in nothing other than the presumption that these transactions have been voluntarily agreed upon by the parties involved. In his 1963 presidential address "What Should Economists Do?" to the Southern Economic Association, Buchanan suggested that the connection, inherent in the concept of voluntary exchange, between the agreement criterion and the notion of mutual gains should be recognized as the trademark of the profession's research program:

> This mutuality of advantage that can be secured … as the result of cooperative arrangements, be these simple or complex, is the one important truth in our discipline (1964: 218, Chapter 26 in this volume).[178]

In order to emphasize this research focus it would be preferable, Buchanan argues, for the discipline to be renamed accordingly:

> Should I have my say, I should propose that we cease, forthwith, to talk about "economics" … Were it possible to wipe the slate clean, I should recommend that we take up a wholly different term such as "catallactics," or "symbiotics." … Symbiotics is defined as the study of the association between dissimilar organisms, and the connotation of the term is that the association is mutually beneficial to all parties. This conveys, more or less precisely, the idea that should be central to our discipline. It draws attention to a unique sort of relationship, that which involves the cooperative association of individuals, one with another, even when individual interests differ (1964: 217, Chapter 26 in this volume).[179]

The catallactics approach, or as he calls it, the *gains-from-trade paradigm*, has in Buchanan's account the virtue of providing a theoretical perspective that can be extended or generalized from the most elementary barter trade to all kinds of cooperative arrangements, however complex, through which the participants realize mutual benefits.[180] As Buchanan notes:

The emphasis shifts, directly and immediately, to all processes of voluntary agreement among persons. ... By a more-or-less natural extension of the catallactics approach, economists can look on politics, and on political process, in terms of the exchange paradigm ([1983] 2000: 17).

Most importantly, the exchange or gains-from-trade paradigm allows, as indicated, the integration of the study of markets and of politics – or, more generally, of decentralized exchange networks and of deliberately organized cooperation – into one coherent theoretical framework.[181] It implies "that 'political exchange,' at all levels, is basically equivalent to economic exchange" (Buchanan and Tullock 1962: 250),[182] and views the political mechanism "as a means through which individuals may cooperate to secure mutually desired ends" (ibid.: 90). As Buchanan elaborates:

> If we adhere strictly to the individualistic benchmark, there can be no fundamental distinction between economics and politics, or more generally, between the economy and the polity. ... Politics, in this individualistic framework, becomes a complex exchange process, in which individuals accomplish purposes collectively that they cannot accomplish non-collectively or privately in any tolerably efficient manner. The catallactic perspective on simple exchange of economic goods merges into the contractarian perspective on politics and political order ([1988] 2001a: 62).

In speaking of the "contractarian perspective," Buchanan makes the claim that, from a choice-individualist approach, the *ultimate* normative criterion in judging "politics and political order" can be no other than the voluntary consent of the individual members of the polity. Applying this criterion at the level of politics is, as he insists, nothing more than a consistent extension of the economist's standard outlook on market transactions to the political realm:

> The political analogue to decentralized trading among individuals must be that feature common over all exchanges, which is *agreement* among the individuals who participate. The unanimity rule for collective choice is the political analogue to freedom of exchange of partitionable goods in markets (1987: 247, Chapter 38 in this volume).

The claim that the notion of voluntary exchange, traditionally applied in the study of markets, can be extended to the realm of politics invites obvious objections, in anticipation of which Buchanan states:

> But how can ordinary politics as we observe it possibly be modeled as a complex exchange process in which individuals *voluntarily* participate, at least in any sense at all analogous to their participation in markets? ... Coercion rather than voluntary participation seems to be the primary relationship embodied in politics. ... A way out of the apparent paradox is provided if we shift attention from ordinary politics, which is almost necessarily majoritarian, or, more generally, nonconsensual in its operation, to constitutional politics, which may at least approach consensual agreement, at least in its idealization. ... The question of legitimacy shifts directly to the rules, to the constitutional structure, which must remain categorically distinct from the operation of ordinary politics ([1988] 2001a: 62f.).

There are obvious differences between the bilateral *exchange contracts* upon which the decentralized network of market-transactions rests and the multilateral or inclusive *social contracts* that constitute political communities or, more generally, systems of deliberately organized cooperation. The exchanges that the latter types of contracts involve can be characterized as exchanges of commitments through which the members of a polity – or, more generally, an organization – mutually submit to binding rules, tied to the membership status. And the mutual benefits they expect in return are the fruits predicted to result from their compliance with these rules. In such joint commitments, Buchanan notes,

> individuals choose to impose constraints or limits on their own behavior ... as a part of an *exchange* in which the restrictions on their own actions are sacrificed in return for the benefits that are anticipated from reciprocally extended restrictions on the actions of others with whom they interact (1990: 4).[183]

By way of illustration he points out:

> In the market, individuals exchange apples for oranges; in politics, individuals exchange agreed-on shares in contributions towards the costs of that which is commonly desired, from the services of the local fire station to that of the judge (1987: 246, Chapter 38 in this volume).[184]

Yet, the difference between the types of exchanges, and their contractual complements, that characterize the two arenas, markets and politics, does not change the fact that, from a choice-individualist perspective, in political exchange no less than in market exchange agreement is the source of legitimacy and the ultimate test of efficiency. As Buchanan insists:

> Individuals acquiesce in the coercion of the state, of politics, only if the ultimate constitutional "exchange" furthers their interests. Without some model of exchange, no coercion of the individual by the state is consistent with the individualistic value norm upon which a liberal social order is grounded (1987: 246, Chapter 38 in this volume).

With its exchange model of politics, with its characterization of political exchange as a social contract, and with its emphasis on agreement as the source of legitimacy, the research program of constitutional political economy finds its place in the tradition of social contract theories of the state.[185] In Buchanan's view, theorists who have rejected "the contract theory of the state as an explanation of either the origin or the basis of political society ... have tended to overlook those elements within the contractarian tradition that do provide us with the 'bridge' between the individual-choice calculus and group decisions" (Buchanan and Tullock 1962: vii).

> One of the primary purposes of the contract theorists of political order seems to have been that of reducing the logic of collective organization to a logic of individual calculus, or, stated differently, of deriving the logic ... for collective organization from the individual-choice situation (ibid.: 316).[186]

Buchanan notes in particular the affinity of his approach to political economy with John Rawls' modern restatement of social contract theory.[187] Rawls' *Theory of Justice* is indeed in important respects similar to Buchanan's contractarianism, but there are also relevant differences. It is instructive to take a closer look at the commonalities and differences between the two versions of modern contractarianism, a task to which the remainder of this section shall be devoted.

Regarding the mixture of affinities and differences that he sees between his own approach and Rawls' contractarianism, Buchanan notes that he was more sympathetic with Rawls' original concept of "justice as fairness" (Rawls 1957, Chapter 25 in this volume) than with the later expanded book version of his theory (Rawls 1971).[188] The affinities between Buchanan's and Rawls' contractarian approaches can be clearly recognized when one looks at how the latter states the core assumptions of his early theory:

> Consider a society where certain practices are already established, and whose members are mutually self-interested: their allegiance to the established practices is founded on the prospect of self-advantage. … Imagine also that the persons in this society are rational: they know their own interests more or less accurately; they are capable of tracing out the likely consequences of adopting one practice rather than another and of adhering to a decision once made. … Now suppose that on some particular occasion several members of this society come together to discuss … the principles by which complaints, and so practices themselves, are to be judged. … They understand further that the principles proposed and acknowledged on this occasion are to be binding on future occasions. Thus, each will be wary of proposing principles which give him a peculiar advantage … since he will be bound by it in future cases the circumstances of which are unknown and in which the principle might well be to his detriment. Everyone is, then, forced to make in advance a firm commitment, which others also may reasonably be expected to make, and no one is able to tailor the canons of a legitimate complaint to fit his own special condition (Rawls 1957: 655f., Chapter 25 in this volume).

This description of a contractual arrangement is meant, as Rawls notes, to bring

> out the idea that fundamental to justice is the concept of fairness which relates to right dealings between persons who are cooperating with or competing against one another, as when one speaks of fair games, fair competition, and fair bargain (ibid.: 657).

In the same sense in which Buchanan speaks of the normative premise of *individual sovereignty*, Rawls notes:

> The peculiar feature of the concept of justice is that it treats each person as an equal sovereign, as it were, and requires a unanimous acknowledgment from a certain original position of equal liberty (Rawls 1963: 124).

And just as Buchanan views the catallactics perspective or the gains-from-trade paradigm as a corollary of the premise of individual sovereignty, Rawls locates the "most fundamental idea" of his contractarian concept of justice in "the idea of citizens (those engaged in cooperation) as free and equal persons" (Rawls 2001: 5), and in "the idea of society as a fair system of social cooperation" (ibid.). It is a concept of justice that can "provide an acceptable philosophical and moral basis for democratic institutions" (ibid.) and for democratic society as a "cooperative venture for mutual advantage" (Rawls 1971: 84).[189]

While the above-described elements of Rawls' theory of justice are surely compatible with Buchanan's contractarianism, the theory's expanded version introduces modifications that set Rawls' contractarianism clearly apart from Buchanan's. Instead of speaking of a social contract as an agreement among persons who know who they are, but are uncertain about how, over time, they will be affected by the "rules of the game" they are to choose, Rawls now conceives the social contract as an agreement concluded among fictitious persons in a fictitious original position in which they have no knowledge whatsoever of who they will be once the "rules of the game" they are to choose will become effective. In Rawls' words:

> In justice as fairness the original position of equality corresponds to the state of nature in the traditional theory of the social contract. … It is understood as a purely hypothetical situation characterized so as to lead to a certain conception of justice. Among the essential features of this situation is that no one knows his place in society, his class position or social status, nor does any one know his fortune in the distribution of natural assets and abilities, his intelligence, strength, and the like. … The principles of justice are chosen behind a veil of ignorance. … Since all are similarly situated and no one is able to design principles to favor his particular condition, the principles of justice are the result of a fair agreement or bargain (1971: 12).

In Buchanan's contractarianism, in contrast, it is the actual agreement among actual persons that counts as a criterion of legitimacy and as a test of efficiency in social matters. For this purpose, for which references to hypothetical agreements among fictitious persons in an original position can obviously be of no help, the relevant point of reference is, as Buchanan has often pointed out, the here and now, the status quo, in which the contracting persons find themselves (Vanberg 2004). In this sense Buchanan notes:

> Obviously time is wasted if discussion is limited to a hypothetical group of individuals considering the original organization of a political society. The interpretation of the contract theory as applying to such a situation has, I think, plagued much of the critical discussion of this theory, and it has obscured the basic validity of the contract approach (1966: 31).[190]

Directly related to his invoking the hypothetical original position is a second feature of Rawls' later theory that sets it apart from Buchanan's contractarianism. For Buchanan the essential virtue of the contractarian perspective is that it focuses evaluative attention on the procedure by which decisions are made rather than on the outcome of these decisions per se. For Rawls the very purpose of introducing the construct of the original position is that it may serve as a device that allows the determination of the *content* of the agreement that rational persons can be predicted to conclude under the conditions so specified. As Rawls states:

> In working out the conception of justice one main task clearly is to determine which principles of justice would be chosen in the original position. To do this we must describe this situation in some detail and formulate with care the problem of choice which it presents (1971: 14).

For Buchanan the purpose of the contractarian outlook is to determine the requirements real world decision procedures must meet in order for the outcomes they produce, whatever they may be, to qualify as legitimate and efficient in terms of the agreement criterion.

One of the principles that, according to Rawls, rational persons would agree upon in the original position[191] is the so-called difference principle which requires that "social and economic inequalities are to be arranged so that they are ... to the greatest benefit of the least advantaged" (1971: 302). It is in particular this principle that has been the subject of much of the discussion on Rawls' theory, and it is of interest in the present context to take a brief look at the role that this principle plays in the contrast between Harsanyi's above-described "equiprobability model" and Rawls' contractarianism.

As mentioned above (fn. 95), Harsanyi contrasts his model with Rawls' "veil of ignorance," noting that his theory is decidedly utilitarian while Rawls draws "very nonutilitarian conclusions." What both outlooks have in common is that they aim at predicting what rules or principles rational persons would agree upon when placed in a situation in which they are unable to foresee how they will be personally affected by the rules or principles chosen. Both reduce or redefine, in effect, the problem of *different persons* coming to an agreement as being a problem of rational choice faced by a *single person*, a "representative" individual.[192] After all, due to the assumptions implied in Harsanyi's equiprobability model as well as in Rawls' veil-of-ignorance assumption, the persons that are supposed to come to an agreement are perfectly identical.[193]

Harsanyi and Rawls differ in the conclusions they draw from their respective hypothetical constructs, in their claims about what would be rational to choose under the presumed conditions of ignorance. While in Rawls' view the difference principle would be opted for, Harsanyi, as reported above (section 3.4), claims that truly rational persons would rather decide in favor of maximizing expected utility.[194] In contrast to both, Buchanan's contractarianism is about actual agreements among a plurality of individuals, agreements about the content of which the observing economist may merely pronounce conjectures, conjectures that are subject to the test of agreement actually forthcoming.

5.4 Gains-From-Trade Paradigm, Maximization Paradigm, and Collective Rationality

The catallactics approach or gains-from-trade paradigm that Buchanan advocates, he contrasts with the *maximization* paradigm that, in his judgment, is "the fatal methodological flaw in modern economics" (1979: 281).[195] What Buchanan refers to as "the distinction between a gains-from-trade or exchange perspective and an allocational or maximizing perspective" ([1988] 2001b: 137) is reflected in fundamentally different theoretical concepts for how to move "from the individual to the collective level of choice" (1990: 11). While the exchange or catallactics approach generalizes or transfers the notion of *mutual gains* from the level of individuals' transactions in markets to the level of collective choice in deliberately organized cooperation, the allocational or maximization approach seeks to bridge the gap between the two levels by generalizing or transferring the notion of *utility maximizing choice* from the level of individual action to units of collective action.

According to Buchanan, part of the blame for the, in his view, inappropriate transfer of the maximization notion from individual to collective action goes to Lionel Robbins' (1932: 16) influential definition of economics as "a science which studies human behavior as a relationship between ends and scarce means which have alternative uses."[196] This definition of the "economic problem" suggests, Buchanan charges, conceiving of economics "as a varied set of exercises, all of which involve the maximization of some appropriately selected objective function subject to appropriately defined constraints" ([1976] 2001: 125), a conception that leaves open as to which entity it is that confronts the "economic problem." It is thus, Buchanan posits,

> by quite natural extension that the economic problem moves from that one which is confronted by the individual person to that facing the larger family group, the business firm, the trade union, the trade association, the church, the local community, the regional or state government, the national government, and, finally, the world (1964: 214, Chapter 26 in this volume).[197]

In the wake of the methodological consensus that emerged in "the post-Robbins era" (Buchanan [1979] 1999: 256), it were, in particular, the welfare economists who explicitly extended the "model of the individual maximizer to ... the community or collectivity as a unit" (ibid.), an extension that, so Buchanan charges, amounts to the "implicit presumption that collectivities choose analogously to individuals" (Buchanan 1990: 6).

That treating collectivities as quasi-individuals means "to bring some organic conception in by the back door" (Buchanan and Tullock 1962: 13), and that in doing so welfare economists in effect abandon the individualistic premises which they otherwise consider an essential attribute of their discipline, has been noted by other authors as well. John Rawls, who views his contractarian theory as a paradigmatic alternative to a utilitarian outlook as it survives in welfare economics, argues for instance:

> It is customary to think of utilitarianism as individualistic, and certainly there are good reasons for this. ... Yet utilitarianism is not individualistic ... in that, by conflating all systems of desires, it applies to society the principle of choice for one man (Rawls 1971: 29).[198]

In a similar sense in which Buchanan contrasts the exchange and the maximization paradigm, Rawls notes:

> Implicit in the contrasts between classical utilitarianism and justice as fairness is a difference in the underlying conception of society. In the one we think of a well-ordered society as a scheme of cooperation for reciprocal advantage ..., in the other as the efficient administration of social resources to maximize the satisfaction of the system of desire constructed by the impartial spectator from the many individual systems of desires accepted as given (ibid.: 33).

Rutledge Vining (1956: 36, Chapter 8 in this volume) has likewise accused welfare economists of confusing "the problem of political economy with the technical means-end problem" by inappropriately regarding "the entire society as a 'task-oriented group'" (ibid.: 34), and supposing "some will or decision-maker who controls the activities of the group directed toward the objective" (ibid.).

An early critic of the *"normative-teleological thinking"* exemplified by welfare economics was Gunnar Myrdal ([1922] 1953: 21, Chapter 2 in this volume), who objected to the notion of society as an evaluating entity, saying that "there does not exist such 'valuation' (in the singular) in the market or in society. There are as many valuations as there are persons engaged in exchange" (ibid.). The notion of a "general welfare" is, Myrdal argued, "identical with the notion of the economic process as a form of collective housekeeping in the interests of society" (ibid.: 16);[199] a notion that he derides as "communistic fiction" ([1922] 1953: 194), that is, the tacit assumption "that there is such a thing as the interest of society as a whole" (ibid.: 195).[200] It is noteworthy that in his 1956 article on "Social Indifference Curves" Paul Samuelson has voiced similar critical arguments without, however, drawing the inferences that these arguments would seem to suggest for his own construct of a social welfare function. Speaking of the "dubious analogy with the single-man's indifference curves" (Samuelson 1956: 2), Samuelson lists the following conceivable defenses of "the use of community indifference curves for a country or a group of individuals" (ibid.: 3):

- to claim "that our country is inhabited by Robinson Crusoe alone,"
- to assume that the country is "a totalitarian nation" and to equate the dictator's indifference curve with that of the community,
- to claim "that our nation is inhabited by a number of identical individuals with identical tastes" (ibid.).

None of these defenses, though, Samuelson concludes, "succeeds in providing a justification of the existence and the use of community indifference curves" (ibid.: 4). Noting that "when we come to the group case it is the essence of the problem that values may differ" (ibid.: 4, fn. 9), Samuelson arrives at the verdict:

> Logically, therefore, it will be as hard or easy to draw up community indifference curves for the whole world as to do it for any subgroup of individuals (ibid.: 3).

Just as it is a core ingredient of welfare economics, the maximization paradigm is equally at the core of a social choice theory that invokes the concept of *collective rationality* as a standard for judging policy decisions.[201] In his seminal *Social Choice and Individual Values* Arrow explicitly stated that in

> analogy with the usual utility analysis of the individual consumer ... rational behavior on the part of the community would mean that the community orders ... alternatives according to its collective preferences ... and then chooses ... that alternative ... which stands highest on this list (Arrow [1951] 1963: 2).

He adds:

> If we continue the traditional identification of rationality with maximization of some sort ..., then the problem of achieving a social maximum derived from individual desires is precisely the problem which has been central to the field of welfare economics (ibid.: 3).

As noted above (section 4.1), with his "impossibility theorem" that has attracted so much attention Arrow claims to have shown that there are no "methods of aggregating individual tastes which imply rational behavior on the part of the community and which will be satisfactory in other ways" (ibid.).

His reaction to Arrow's 1951 book, which he voiced in his 1954 article "Social Choice,

Democracy, and Free Markets," Buchanan ([1968] 2000: 7) has described in retrospect as "intuitive dissatisfaction," noting that it "directly stimulated" him to develop his own economic outlook at politics. As he recalls:

> My own initial reaction to Arrow's work was, and remains, one of non-surprise. Who would have expected any social process to yield a consistent ordering of results? Only economists who made the critical methodological error of crossing the bridge from individual to social maximization without having recognized what they are doing would have experienced intellectual-ideological disappointment ([1975] 2001: 81).[202]

The paradox to which, as Arrow shows, attempts to aggregate individual preference orderings lead is, in Buchanan's view,

> Disturbing only to those who seek uniqueness in outcome, who seek to impose the maximization paradigm on a social interaction process where it does not belong. By contrast, to those who accept the contractarian paradigm, who seek only to explain and to understand the behavior of persons who interact, one with another, there is nothing disturbing in the paradox ([1979] 1999: 256).[203]

In his 1954 article Buchanan has challenged Arrow's use of the concept of collective rationality as ascribing to a social group "an organic existence apart from that of its individual components" (1954: 116, Chapter 19 in this volume), contrasting such "organic" philosophical outlook with one that adopts the "philosophical bases of individualism in which the individual is the only entity possessing ends or values" (ibid.), an outlook in which "no question of social or collective rationality may be raised" (ibid.).[204] Arrow has only very briefly responded to this challenge, showing no sign of considering Buchanan's argument calling for serious consideration (Arrow 1963: 107). Instead, he insists:

> Collective rationality in the social choice mechanism is not then merely an illegitimate transfer from the individual to society, but an important attribute of a genuinely democratic system capable of full adaptation to varying environments (ibid.: 120).[205]

Arrow's inability or unwillingness to appreciate Buchanan's challenge has to do, I submit, with the paradigmatic divide between his preference-individualism and Buchanan's choice-individualism. For Arrow, the "social choice mechanism" in a "democratic system" has to solve the problem of amalgamating individual preference into a social preference that can guide policy choice. When he speaks of his impossibility theorem proving that "the doctrine of voters' sovereignty is incompatible with that of collective rationality" (Arrow [1951] 1963: 60), he means that, while democracy requires respecting individuals' preferences, there is no method of aggregation that meets rationality requirements. By contrast, for Buchanan's choice- individualism the collective-choice mechanism in a democratic system has to solve the problem of deriving policy decisions from the choices of the ultimate sovereigns, the citizens-members of the polity. Or, stated differently, the task is to organize the political process in ways that, on the one hand, respect the authority of the individual citizens as sovereigns and ultimate source of legitimacy and, on the other hand, allow the polity to function. This task naturally focuses the political economist's attention on the rules and institutions of politics rather than on the evaluation of "social states" as the presumed objects of collective choice. As Buchanan puts it:

> As proofs of the logical inconsistencies in voting rules are acknowledged, as the costs of securing agreement among persons in groups with differing preferences are accounted for, the theory of rules, or of constitutions, emerges almost automatically on the agenda for research ([1978] 2000: 52).

5.5   Constitutionalism: The Choice of Rules

When the Pareto criterion was adopted in order to remedy the shortcomings of the "old" welfare economics it did not take long for its own limitations to become apparent: its rather limited practical applicability. Requiring "unanimous individual preferences" (Sen 1987: 382) for policy measures to qualify as "welfare improving" it allows the political economist to pass judgment only in those presumably extremely rare cases in which policy measures have no distributional effects. Quite obviously, the Wicksellian unanimity criterion can be criticized on the same grounds. Just as a "unanimity of preferences" will rarely prevail in policy matters, a "unanimity of votes" is equally unlikely.[206]

Recognizing its limitations, Wicksell ([1896] 1958: 92, Chapter 24 in this volume) found it necessary to moderate the demands of his criterion, speaking of "the requirement of approximate unanimity of decisions – absolute unanimity may have to be ruled out for practical reasons." Such a concession would seem, though, to be somewhat ad hoc and to considerably weaken the analytical rigor of the unanimity criterion as a research tool in political economy. It is Buchanan's merit that he gave a systematic answer to the practicability challenge by re-interpreting Wicksellian unanimity as a criterion that finds its relevant application not at the level of ordinary policy choices but at the *constitutional level*, at the level where the rules for making ordinary policy choices are chosen.[207]

Wicksell's argument in support of the unanimity criterion had been that, if a public project does indeed increase the welfare of the community, it should be theoretically possible to find a scheme for allocating the financial burden in such a way that assures a net-advantage for everyone and that, accordingly, could find unanimous approval.[208] The reason for the impracticality of working out a cost-distribution scheme that meets this requirement is, as Buchanan points out, easy to see:

> Under a genuine rule of unanimity, individuals will be led to invest resources in strategic bargaining, investment which will, in the net, prove wasteful to the group as a whole. ... Under unanimity some agreement might ultimately be reached at each stage on the way to a final outcome, but serious resource wastage might occur, the most important element of which would be measured in the costs of delaying agreement. Decision-making in groups, bargaining, is a costly process at best, and costs may become prohibitively high under a rule of unanimity, despite the acknowledged relevance of the rule ([1967] 1999: 288).[209]

Considering the impracticability or, in more neutral terms, the costs of deciding policy issues by unanimity, the members of a polity – or, more generally, of any cooperative organization – will have rational reasons to agree on decision-making rules that allow ordinary policy choices to be made by less-than-unanimity, such as simple or qualified majority rules. By doing so they sacrifice the veto-power a unanimity rule would grant them and, thus, accept the risk of decisions being made that go against their interests; they can expect, however, to be compensated by the advantages a functioning political decision-making process promises in which projects they favor have a chance of being implemented.[210] The balancing of the expected benefits and costs that the constituents of a polity have to make when they want the political process to operate is the subject of Buchanan and Tullock's classic in public choice theory and founding contribution to constitutional political economy, *The Calculus of Consent – Logical Foundations of Constitutional Democracy* (1962). About this joint project, Buchanan has noted in retrospect:

> Our procedure was to shift backwards, to the level of choice among rules, the Wicksellian unanimity or general consensus criterion. The transaction costs barrier may be fully acknowledged at the stage of reaching collective decisions on specific fiscal (tax and spending) variables. But this need not imply that persons cannot agree generally on the rules or institutions under which subsequent decisions will be made, whether these will be majority rule or otherwise. To the extent that individuals' future preference positions are uncertain and unpredictable under subsequent operation of rules to be chosen, they may be led to agree on the basis of general criteria that are unrelated to economic positions ([1975] 2000: 13).[211]

The prospects for reaching agreement at the constitutional level in cases in which distributional conflicts rule out agreement at the level of single policy decisions are based on, and limited by, the participants' uncertainty about how they will be personally affected by future applications of rules that are supposed to be in force over an extended period. Choosing behind a "veil of uncertainty," individuals will be induced to evaluate alternative rules in terms of "generalizable criteria of fairness, making agreement more likely to occur than when separable interests are more easily identifiable" (1987: 248, Chapter 38 in this volume).[212]

The distinction between sub-constitutional choices, choices *within* rules, and constitutional choices, choices *of* rules, is central to the research program of constitutional political economy. The distinction applies to any two adjacent levels within a multi-tier system of collective decision-making, such as a federal political system with local, state and national government, or to social systems with rules constraining particular choices, rules for changing these rules, rules for changing rules for changing rules, and so forth.[213] The choice-individualist paradigm allows for less-than-unanimous decisions and for the delegation of decision-making authority to agents, but requires that such practices be legitimized by agreement at the ultimate constitutional level (Buchanan and Tullock 1962: 77, 286f.).[214] As noted above, in spite of conflicting interests, in particular instances individuals will be able to agree to rules for dealing with certain types of issues if, and to the extent that, they are uncertain about how they will be personally affected in unknown future cases. Accordingly, since with increasing generality of rules the veil of uncertainty tends to thicken, the prospects for agreement to be reached increase as one moves upwards in a decision-making hierarchy, with the ultimate constitutional level being most favored in this regard.

Shifting decisions from the level of particular choices to the constitutional level – or, more generally, to move upward to a higher level of a constitutional hierarchy – can serve as a strategy for dealing with issues on which, due to distributional conflicts, consensual solutions cannot be achieved at the given level of choice. As Buchanan argues:

> It is necessary to distinguish sharply between day-to-day political decision making, where the struggle often does reduce simply to that among conflicting individual-group interests, and "constitutional" decision making, where individuals may be thought of as participants in choices of rules under which subsequent day-to-day decisions are to be made. ... [A]t this stage, it becomes possible to reconcile separate individual interests with something that could, with some legitimacy, be called the "public interest" were it not for the confusion that this particular usage might generate (1966: 29).[215]

It is noteworthy that this "constitutional" method for dealing with distributional conflicts has been indirectly invoked in discussions on the practicability of the Kaldor–Hicks compensation criterion. As noted before, this criterion was meant to overcome the inherent limitation the Pareto criterion faces due to the fact that policy measures usually have distributional effects. Yet, it was soon recognized that this supposed remedy has its own limits of applicability. As for example Little (1957: 94) has pointed out, the question "Why not compensate all loosers?" finds an easy answer: "We could not, in practice, find out who has lost and how much would be required to compensate them."[216]

In response to the diagnosed impracticability of case-by-case compensation, it has been suggested that, if used in a modified form, the compensation argument can still support claims that policies such as free trade – the issue which started the debate on the possibility of a value- free welfare economics (see section 3.2) – or free competition are welfare enhancing. Even though in each particular instance such policies produce gainers and losers, it was argued, over time the balance of gains and losses will be such that everybody gains. In this sense Hicks (1941: 111) defended his claim that a "reorganization of production" can be judged "an unequivocal improvement" if the beneficiary *A* could compensate *B* for his loss, arguing:

> If the economic activity of a community were organized on the principle of making ... all alterations which were improvements [in this sense] ..., then, although we could not say that all inhabitants of that community would be necessarily better off than they would have been if the community had been organized on some different principle, nevertheless there would be a strong probability that almost all of them would be better off after the lapse of a sufficient length of time (ibid.).

As Scitovsky (1951: 308, Chapter 7 in this volume) has pointed out, a similar argument had been made by Hotelling,[217] who conceived economic policy

> as a succession of many small changes, each of which would ... distribute welfare in a random fashion. If this were so, the successive redistributions would cancel each other out and leave the improvement in efficiency as the net result, so that everybody would be better off in the end.

In reference to arguments of this kind, Samuelson (1981: 227) speaks of a "tacit dependence" upon a "heuristic theorem," which he describes as follows:

> Most technical changes or policy choices directly help some people and hurt others. For some

changes, it is possible for the winners to buy off the losers so that everyone could conceivably end up better off than in the prior status quo. Suppose that no such compensatory side payments are made, but assume that we are dealing with numerous inventions and policy decisions that are quasi-independent. Even if for each single change it is hard to know in advance who will be helped and who will be hurt, in the absence of known "bias" in the whole sequence of changes, there is some vague presumption that a hazy version of the law of large numbers will obtain: so as the number of quasi-independent events becomes larger and larger, the chances improve that any random person will be on balance benefited by a social compact that lets events take place that push out society's possibility frontier, even though any one of the events may push some people along the new frontier in a direction less favorable than the status quo (ibid.).[218]

Samuelson's attempt, as he characterizes it, "to model the actual thought processes economists muddled through some four decades back" (Samuelson 1981: 227), can be translated into the choice-individualist language of constitutional economics as the claim that, in cases in which a *general compensation* can be reasonably expected under the operation of certain rules or procedures, the individual members of the community in question should be able to agree on such rules or procedures even though they can anticipate that in particular instances they may work against their interests.[219] Proposals for rules or procedures that the political economist advances on the ground that they promise such general compensation, and that he submits as hypothetical imperatives to the community, are, to be sure, subject to the *ultimate* test of finding general agreement among the constituents, or to the proximate test of being accepted in the ordinary political process.[220]

The subjectivist, choice-individualist perspective – requiring the political economist to respect individuals as sovereigns – directs, as Buchanan stresses, the evaluative focus necessarily to the procedures through which social outcomes are reached rather than to these outcomes per se.

> The focus of evaluative attention becomes the process itself, as contrasted with end-state or outcome patterns. "Improvement" must, therefore, be sought in reforms in process, institutional change that will allow the operation of politics to mirror more accurately that set of results that are preferred by those who participate. One way of stating the difference between the Wicksellian approach and that which is still orthodoxy in normative economics is to say that the constitution of policy rather than policy itself becomes the relevant object for reform (1987: 247, Chapter 38 in this volume).[221]

The task of the political economist is seen in "locating possible flaws in the existing social structure and in presenting possible 'improvements'" (1959: 137, Chapter 10 in this volume).[222] Put differently, his social role is seen in "securing more intelligent legislation" (ibid.: 124) in the sense in which Adam Smith ([1776] 1981: 468) defined political economy as "the science of a legislator." The measuring rod for what may count as "more intelligent legislation" or as "improvement" in the institutional structure is the degree to which they enhance the prospects for the individuals involved to realize mutual gains, in terms of what they themselves count as gains. This means, as Buchanan states, that institutions must be designed so that individual behavior will further the interests of the group, small or large, local or national. The challenge to us is one of constructing, or reconstructing, a political order that will channel the self-serving behavior of participants towards the common good in a manner that comes as close as possible to that described for us by Adam Smith with respect to the economic order ([1978] 2000: 53f.).[223]

From the choice-individualist perspective of constitutional political economy, the general aim of institutional reform should be to secure and enhance the authority of individuals as ultimate sovereigns. For the *constitution of markets* this can be operationalized in terms of the principle of *consumers' sovereignty*, for the *constitution of politics* in terms of the principle of *citizens' sovereignty*.[224] It must be kept in mind, though, that while the two forms of individual sovereignty serve as performance criteria for their respective domains, they are not equally foundational. What consumers' sovereignty entails is defined by the rules that constitute markets as arenas for voluntarily agreed on transactions. The *constitutions* of markets, however, can derive their legitimacy not from the voluntary agreements concluded *within* their arenas, but only from *constitutional* agreement among the members of the relevant community.[225] On the other hand, and for the same reason, non-unanimous decisions in politics do not de-legitimize the democratic process, as long as the rules that allow for such decisions are legitimized by agreement at the constitutional level. In this sense Buchanan ([1991] 1999: 288) says about "the normative premise that individuals are the ultimate sovereigns in matters of social organization":

> In accordance with this premise, the legitimacy of social organizational structures is to be judged against the voluntary agreement of those who are to live or are living under the arrangements that are judged. The central premise of *individuals as sovereigns* does allow for delegation of decision-making authority to agents, so long as it remains understood that individuals remain as *principals*. The premise denies legitimacy to all social-organizational arrangements that negate the role of individuals as either sovereigns or principals. On the other hand, the normative premise of individuals as sovereigns does not provide exclusive normative legitimacy to organizational structures that – as, in particular, market institutions – allow internally for the most extensive range of separate individual choice. Legitimacy must also be extended to "choice-restricting" institutions so long as the participating individuals voluntarily choose to live under such regimes (ibid.).

5.6   The Game Analogy and the "Choice of Social States"

On various occasions Buchanan has acknowledged that in developing his contractarian-constitutionalist research program he had been strongly influenced by Frank Knight, with whom he studied at the University of Chicago, and by Rutledge Vining, also a student of Knight, who had been his colleague at the University of Virginia.[226] It was, as he reports, in particular the game analogy as "an approach to political economy" (1959: 133, fn. 11, Chapter 10 in this volume) that he took from Knight and especially from Vining.[227]

Emphasizing the "parallelism between play and political and economic life," Knight ([1946] 1982: 466) had posited that "it is useful to think of social life as a game" (ibid.: 455), in the sense that the "first characteristic of play, as of all social activity, ... is that freedom is conditioned and limited by 'law', in several meanings of the word" (ibid.: 464). A main task of the political economist he saw as assisting in the choice of the "'rules of the game', in the shape of law for economic relationships" (Knight 1940: 28).

Following Knight's lead,[228] Vining advocated a political economy in the spirit of Adam Smith's "science of the legislator" (Vining 1969: 199).[229] Such a political economy, he notes, inquires "into the nature of certain fundamental concepts that are inherent in an actual situation in which a group of persons jointly decide upon a legislative program" (ibid.), or, in other words, it deals with the kinds of problems that are faced by individuals who "jointly choose the constraints and regulations which they impose on their individual actions" (Vining 1956: 9).[230] Such problems, Vining (1969: 200) supposes, can be usefully looked at in analogy to "a group of players of a game who will have stopped their play in order to consider certain proposed modifications of the rules of the game." As he argues:

> [T]he economic problem is posed when members of the society are induced by what they observe to inquire into the possibility of improving the performance of the system currently in force. ... We are using the term "economic system" to mean a system of legislative constraints upon individual action. In the sense that laws and regulations are rules, an economic system is a system of rules, and legislators are confronted always with the problem of finding a better-working system of rules (Vining 1956: 14).[231]

Contrasting his theoretical outlook with a welfare economics that interprets politics as an optimization problem, Vining (1984: 30, fn. 12, Chapter 37 in this volume) insists that "the notion of a well-defined objective test of optimality" is not applicable to "a group of persons in the act of choosing (i.e. of reaching agreement upon) a criterion of choice – to be routinely applied, say, in actions subsequently to be taken on the group's behalf" (ibid.).[232] As he puts it:

> The members of the society must reach a consensus, and the choice is based upon a joint evaluation. This involves the resolution of conflicting evaluations through argument and discussion. ... The system must be jointly chosen by the members of the society, and the technical problem, beyond the measurement and prediction of performance characteristics, is that of facilitating the social inter-action and communication leading to a consensus (Vining 1956: 18).[233]

The game analogy, suggested to him by Knight and Vining, Buchanan embraced as an analytical tool congenial to his contractarian-constitutionalist view. It allows, in particular, the illustration of the critical distinction between the two levels of choice, the choice *within* rules and the choice of rules,[234] and the systematic difference between the participants' interests at the two levels, their potentially conflicting interests in playing a given game successfully, and their common interests in playing a "better" game, a game that is more attractive for all players involved.[235] It is this characteristic combination of commonality and conflict of interests that Knight ([1942] 1982: 249) had emphasized in using the game analogy:

> [P]lay exhibits in relation to its rules or laws the ubiquitous harmony and conflict of interests. All the parties to any game have a common interest in the game itself – hence, in general obedience to the rules. But they have conflicting individual interests in winning – consequently, in law-breaking or cheating. Similar considerations apply far more acutely to the improvement of the game by

changing the rules. The notion of law and its enforcement – and improvement – will be found to be the locus of virtually all social problems.

Knight also pointed out that, while searching for more promising strategies in playing a game is in every player's immediate interest, searching for rules that improve the game for all involved is a common good in which individuals will predictably invest less effort than in the former activity. In his words:

> It is a vitally important fact that the capacity to play intelligently, from the standpoint of winning, is much more highly and commonly developed among human beings than is the capacity to improve or invent better games (Knight [1946] 1982: 466).

The game analogy can not only help to illustrate the distinction between the two levels of choice that is central to the contractarian-constitutionalist research program, it can also help to bring into sharper relief the fundamental contrast between the latter's choice-individualist perspective and the utility- or preference-individualist perspective of welfare economics and social choice theory. At the heart of this contrast is the critical difference between the question of what is the object of choice and the question of what is the object of *evaluation*. Arrow (1996: xiii) points to this distinction when he states: "Choice is over sets of actions, but preference orderings are over consequences."[236] Yet, in the way he defines the project of social choice theory he hardly pays serious attention to the implications that this statement would seem to suggest. In his *Social Choice and Individual Values* he expressly states:

> In the present study the objects of choice are social states. The most precise definition of a social state would be a complete description of the amount of each type of commodity in the hands of each individual, the amount of labor to be supplied by each individual, the amount of each productive resource invested in each type of productive activity, and the amounts of various types of collective activity, such as municipal services, diplomacy and its continuation by other means, and the erection of statues of famous men. It is assumed that each individual in the community has a definite ordering of all conceivable social states, in terms of their desirability to him (Arrow [1951] 1963: 67).[237]

Even if, on occasion, Arrow speaks of each individual having "some way of ranking social actions according to his preference for their consequences" (Arrow 1969: 221, Chapter 20 in this volume), and of "society's choices among alternative social actions" (ibid.: 225),[238] it is apparent that with his social choice theory he aims at judgments about the merits of *social states* among which society supposedly can choose.[239]

The notion of choice among social states is equally invoked

- when Sen (1970: 152) speaks of a *"collective choice rule"* that specifies a social preference ordering based on individuals' orderings "over the set X of all possible social states, each social state being a complete description of society including every individual's position in it,"[240]
- when, according to Bergson (1954: 240), welfare economics is concerned with providing advice for "decisions involving alternative social states," or

• when Samuelson (1967: 42) speaks of choices being made among "alternative states of the world," and when he posits that "given sufficient knowledge the optimal decisions can always be found by scanning over all the attainable states of the world and selecting the one which according to the postulated ethical welfare function is best" (Samuelson 1954: 389).

It is the very notion that politics is about the choice of social states that Vining (1956: 35, Chapter 8 in this volume) chastised as "the confusion in the work of the 'welfare economists',," insisting that social states

> result from millions of individual choices each made under a given system of constraints which apply to all individuals; and it is the system of constraints and not the resulting allocation or distribution which is chosen by the joint action of the individuals constituting the society (ibid.).[241]

The game analogy, as Vining has pointed out, is particularly useful as an illustration of the fact that "social states" as defined by Arrow and Sen cannot be chosen but are the resultant of the choices made by all participants in the social process.[242] In game-like social settings (and these are the settings political economy is typically concerned with), in which individuals are free to make their own choices, nobody chooses outcomes. The players can *evaluate* conceivable outcomes, but they cannot *choose* outcomes. They can only choose among available strategies, while outcomes result from the combination of strategies chosen.[243]

In his 1954 paper "Social Choice, Democracy, and Free Markets" Buchanan had criticized "Arrow's interpretation of 'the market' as a social decision rule" (1995: 141, Chapter 40 in this volume), arguing:

> Market outcomes emerge from the separated but interdependent choice behavior of many actors, and, as emergent rather than explicitly chosen social states, these outcomes are not within the feasible choice set of either separate participants or the collectivity of individuals in the organized community (ibid.: 142).[244]

Looking back after four decades he comments on his earlier assessment:

> I now recognize ... that I accepted the social choice paradigm all too readily, as being applicable to the nonmarket spheres of interaction among individuals. I should have recognized that the very notion of social choice is an analytical mirage, and that "choice" can never be applicable to a selection among social states. Instead, choices are necessarily restricted to selection among alternatives that may be arrayed along a set of dimensions of activity that can never be fully determinate of a social state, even in some conceptual sense (Buchanan 1995: 142, Chapter 40 in this volume).

As long as individuals "retain personal control over actions along at least some minimal set of dimensions of behavioral adjustment" (ibid.), as we must assume they do in virtually all social settings, social states in the sense defined by Arrow and Sen, so Buchanan argues, "cannot be chosen, whether by a single person with authority or by a group of persons who might try to make collective decisions through some rule" (ibid.: 146).[245]

What can be collectively chosen through the political process are policy measures which, contingent on the adaptive responses of the affected individuals, will produce "social states" as outcomes. And the principal instrument to systematically shape the *pattern* of predicted outcomes are changes in the "rules of the game," that is, in the constraints that the institutional framework imposes on the participants' behavioral choices. As Buchanan concludes:

> The result forces a recognition of the elementary fact that the objects of social choice are alternative assignments of rights, or alternative rules structures, rather than alternative social states, although individuals' evaluations of such assignments or structures may depend solely on ultimate evaluations of predicted patterns of emergent outcomes (1995: 149, Chapter 40 in this volume).[246]

As has been repeatedly emphasized above, the focus of the choice-individualist approach of constitutional political economy is on the rules under which, or the *procedures* from which, social outcomes result, and it evaluates these outcomes only *indirectly*, according to the extent to which the *procedures* that generate them allow the individuals involved to realize their own interests in mutually beneficial, or at least in mutually compatible ways.[247] This *procedural* focus has been contrasted with the outcome- or end-state-oriented focus of welfare economics and social choice theory which aim at evaluating outcomes or "social states" *directly*, independently of the nature of the process from which they result.[248] Some clarifying comments on this contrast may be necessary in order to guard against potentially misleading interpretations of what is entailed when Buchanan ([1988] 2001a: 60) posits:

> Normative judgments take the form of statements that array "better" and "worse" *processes* (rules, laws, institutions) ... These judgments are categorically distinct from those that array and evaluate results or outcomes.

Such a misleading interpretation is suggested, for instance, by Sen, when he depicts the contrast between Buchanan's procedural approach and the outcome-focused approach of social choice theory as if it were about consequentialism, that is, about the issue of whether or not choices are judged in light of their predicted consequences. After noting the "consequentialist sympathies" of social choice theory,[249] Sen (1997: 24, Chapter 22 in this volume) notes that this "consequence-centered formulation has recently come under attack from various authors who have opted for giving priority to processes and procedures," and he refers to Buchanan's "early critiques of social choice theory" as pioneering such an attack.[250] Buchanan's "emphasis on procedural judgments," Sen (1995: 2, Chapter 21 in this volume) argues,

> may be taken to suggest ... that we should abandon altogether consequence-based evaluation of social happenings, opting instead for a procedural approach. In its pure form, such an approach would look for "right" institutions rather than "good" outcomes and would demand the priority of appropriate procedures ... This approach ... is the polar opposite to the welfare-economic tradition based on classical utilitarianism of founding every decision on an ordering of different states of affairs (treating procedures just as instruments to generate good states) (ibid.).

While Sen concedes that Buchanan "did not deny the importance of consequential analysis" (1997: 24, Chapter 22 in this volume),[251] and grants that "Buchanan's argument for a more procedural view of social decisions has some merits" (1995: 18, Chapter 21 in this volume), he concludes:

> Nevertheless, there are good reasons to doubt the adequacy of a purely procedural view (independent of consequences), just as there are serious defects in narrowly consequentialist views (independent of procedures) (ibid.).

What is misleading about Sen's comments on Buchanan's procedural focus is the supposition that the issue at stake is whether or not we can "judge procedures adequately in a consequence-independent way" (ibid.: 11). The point of Buchanan's critique of social choice theory's focus on end-states is, however, definitely not to claim that their expected consequences play no role at all in judging procedure.[252] Instead, it is about, firstly, the distinction between what is valued and what can be chosen and, secondly, the distinction between individuals' evaluation of procedures in terms of predicted outcomes, and the economists' assessment of procedures in terms of how well they take account of individuals' evaluations in generating outcomes. Buchanan refers to these distinctions when he posits:

> People may be supposed to place ultimate value on the characteristics of social states that may, first, be imagined, and, second, arrayed in some order of preference. There need be no deontological intrusion that introduces any evaluation of procedures or rules, per se. The approach here implies only that that which is valued cannot, itself, be directly chosen in any meaningfully defined process, whether this be private (individual) or collective. Individuals participate in the choices among assignments of rights, among rules, that, in turn generate social states as participants rationally choose among alternatives within the structure so chosen. Assignments of rights may be valued only as they are predicted to allow for the emergence of valued outcomes. It becomes an empty exercise to evaluate rules independently of the outcomes that are predicted to emerge under their operation. It should be equally empty to evaluate imagined social states without consideration of the structure of rights, or rules, that may be expected to generate them (1995: 146f., Chapter 40 in this volume).

To state the distinction Buchanan implies here more explicitly, the individuals as sovereigns will choose rules in light of their evaluation of predicted working properties, and a main task of the political economist is to inform about these predicted working properties. Yet, as the subjectivist-choice-individualist paradigm implies, the political economist has no way – and no authority – to evaluate *for the individuals* the alternatives among which they as the ultimate sovereigns are to choose. Instead, as observers, political economists are necessarily limited to judging the *procedures* through which such choices are made in terms of the normative premise of individual sovereignty. To be sure, they must base whatever proposals they advance for institutional reforms on assumptions about individuals' presumed evaluations of predicted consequences. But such assumptions cannot be more than *conjectures* – conjectures that remain subject to the test of the individuals concerned actually agreeing.

The principal difference in outlook that is at stake here is between, on the one hand, the insistence, implied in the contractarian-constitutionalist paradigm, on the need to distinguish between the issue of *legitimacy* and the issue of *efficiency* (see section 5.2), and, on the other hand, the tendency in welfare economics and social choice theory to conflate the two. The utility- or preference-individualism of the latter implies that, by "reading" and properly amalgamating individuals' preferences, the political economist answers at the same time the questions of legitimacy and efficiency in collective choice. The choice-individualism of constitutional political economy, by contrast, insists that legitimacy in collective choice can only be derived, directly or indirectly, from agreement among the members-principals of the group in question, while efficiency arguments are about the reasons that may motivate the members-principals to come to an agreement.[253]

With its procedural perspective, constitutional political economy focuses on the legitimacy issue. With their end-state-oriented perspective, welfare economics and social choice theory focus on the efficiency issue. The value of the conjectures that they advance about potentially efficiency-enhancing policy choices the constitutional political economist need not dispute, as long as it is understood that these conjectures can be no more than this, conjectures about the validity of which only the individuals themselves can pass final judgment, not the observing economist.

6   Policy Advice in a Democratic Society

The comparative assessment of the three variants of political economy to which the preceding sections have been devoted, welfare economics, social choice theory and constitutional economics, was based on the presumption that political economy should be looked at as an *applied* rather than a *normative* branch of economics. As an applied science that pronounces *hypothetical* rather than *categorical* imperatives, political economy remains within the limits set for any science that submits its claims to logical examination and empirical testing. Hypothetical imperatives are *conditional* ought-statements; they posit that *if* one wants to achieve some aim Y, measure X can be recommended as a suitable means for doing so. Such conditional ought-statements are factual claims that are falsified if X can be shown not to be able to bring about Y, and that are obviously of relevance only if they are addressed to someone who actually wants to achieve Y.[254]

The kind of advisory role that political economists might assume obviously depends on the nature of the political system within which they seek to offer their services, whether this is a totalitarian state, an autocracy, a representative democracy, or some other kind of political regime. For the variants of political economy considered here, it is obvious that they are meant to serve their role in advising politics in a *democratic* society. As has been shown, they are all based on the premise of a normative individualism (even if differently interpreted, as utility- or preference-individualism in the case of welfare economics and social choice theory, or as choice-individualism in the case of constitutional political economy), and this individualism is typically seen as implying a democratic concept of politics.

In regard to welfare economics, for instance, it is said:

> The assumption that the social welfare function is determined by the utilities of all individuals has been called the fundamental ethical postulate by Samuelson (1947) and is a cornerstone of democratic society (Just, Hueth, Schmitz 2004: 40).

In regard to a social choice theory that views the "social good" as "a composite of the desires of individuals," Arrow ([1951] 1963: 23f.) notes that a "viewpoint of this type serves as a

justification of both political democracy and ... an economic system involving free choice."
In the same sense Sen (2010: 32) speaks of "the democratic foundations of social choice
theory."[255] Most obviously, constitutional political economy "rests squarely on a democratic
foundation" (Buchanan 1990: 15).[256]

If democratic society is the forum in which political economists mean to serve as advisors
in policy matters, there are, in principle, three potential candidates to whom such advice may
be addressed: the citizenry at large, political agents who exercise decision-making authority
on citizens' behalf, or interests groups as sub-sections of the citizenry. To advise the latter on
how to advance their particular interests politics, political economists have typically not
considered as one of their tasks.[257] Of relevance are the citizens as *ultimate* and political agents
as *proximate* addressees.

In addressing citizens at large, such advice, in order to be effective, must appeal to interests
that all members of the polity supposedly share. In addressing political agents it must appeal
to interests that they harbor, which will, first of all, be directed at being successful in the
competition for office to which they are exposed.[258] In ideally working democratic politics, the
constraints of political competition would assure that citizens' common interests and political
agents' interests are perfectly aligned. In actual operation democratic politics will fall short of
such perfect alignment, with the potential for conflict between citizens' common interests and
the immediate interests of political agents.

The preceding comments provide the basis on which welfare economics, social choice
theory and constitutional political economy may now be examined in light of the following
questions:

- To whom are their respective hypothetical imperatives supposed to be addressed?
- Are the measures they suggest suitable means for achieving the hypothesized aim?
- Can the supposed addressees be assumed to have an interest in achieving the hypothesized
  aim?

On reviewing the relevant literature it is apparent that welfare economists have been
notoriously ambiguous as to whom they mean to address whatever advice they have to offer.
In his 1938 contribution to the field, Bergson argued, for instance, that the value proposition
to be included in the social welfare function must be

> determined by its compatibility with the values prevailing in the community the welfare of which
> is being studied. For only if the welfare principles are based upon prevailing values, can they be
> relevant to the activity of the community in question (Bergson 1938: 328).

In a 1954 essay he says about "the criterion of social welfare":

> [T]he values taken as data in counseling any one citizen may be the same as those taken in
> counseling any other. Or they may be different. In the former case, the criterion of social welfare
> is given at once. It is defined simply by the values one would take as data in counseling any
> individual. In the latter case, however, it is necessary still to decide a second question of a
> methodological sort: Whom to counsel? One might still wish to counsel any and all citizens at the
> same time. If so, the criterion is defined only within areas on which the values of all are the same.

> Within this area, the criterion is given by the values held in common. Alternatively one might wish to counsel some select group, which holds some values in common. Here this criterion is given by the value of the group in question (Bergson 1954: 240).[259]

And in a 1976 publication of his one reads:

> [W]elfare economics is envisaged essentially as a form of counselling. The counsel relates to public economic policies affecting social states and might be proffered to citizens generally, but is usually intended especially for public officials. The counsel consists of implications of some criterion of social welfare ... The practitioner of welfare economics is in principle free to take any values as a point of departure, but the resulting counsel as to the economic policy is not apt to be too relevant unless the values in question are held by, or can plausibly be imputed to, one or more officials concerned with the policies in question. Should the practitioner for any reason disapprove of those values, he may, of course, refrain from offering the officials any counsel at all (Bergson 1976: 186).

With the apparent intent so sound provocative, Samuelson, in his textbook's famous chapter on welfare economics, answers the question of whose interests his welfare functions are meant to address in these words:

> Without inquiring into its origins, we take as a starting point for our discussion a function of all the economic magnitudes of a system which is supposed to characterize some ethical belief – that of a benevolent despot, or a complete egoist, or "all men of good will," a misanthrope, the state, race, or group mind, God, etc. Any possible opinion is admissible ... We only require that the belief be such as to admit of an unequivocal answer as to whether one configuration of the economic system is "better" or "worse" than any other or "indifferent," and those relationships are transitive (Samuelson 1947: 221, Chapter 6 in this volume).

Noting that, if welfare economics is to be of relevance, it cannot be based "on a definition of social welfare that appeals to no one," Ng (1979: 5) states in his textbook on the subject:

> Thus, what a welfare economist can do is to use either a concept of social welfare which he himself believes to be the right objective or one that most people or the government believe to be so, or some compromise (ibid.: 6).

As Mishan (1960: 201) has noted,

> welfare propositions rest on both factual and ethical assumptions. Unless both are granted, the first being "realistic," the second being "widely acceptable," the welfare propositions deduced from them are of no practical importance.

It is surely less in regard to the former than to the latter that, as he observes, "[m]any of the modern writers on welfare economics take a poor view of its prospects" (ibid.: 251).[260] Graaff, for instance, whose *Theoretical Welfare Economics* Samuelson (1968: vii) had recommended as reflecting "what modern welfare economics is all about," voiced this view on the issue:

The question of agreement is really fundamental. Let us take it for granted that wide, if not universal, agreement can be obtained on the factual assumptions underlying welfare theory. The possibility of building an interesting theory then hinges on the possibility of obtaining sufficient consilience of opinion on ethical matters to enable specific injunctions to be deduced. Now, clearly, there is some degree of consilience of opinion in any reasonably homogeneous society ... But whether or not the common ground is sufficiently extensive for the purposes of welfare theory is another matter.

... It seems to me extremely improbable that agreement on these basic matters will ever be obtained. And it seems to me, therefore, that the possibility of building a useful and interesting theory of welfare economics – i.e. one which consists of something more than the barren formalisms typified by the marginal equivalences of conventional theory – is exceedingly small (Graaff [1963] 1968: 168f.).

In a more recent comment on the prospects of welfare economics of finding interested addressees for its hypothetical imperatives, Atkinson arrives at an equally sober assessment:

However, many economists are clearly addressing policy-makers, governments and international organizations. If that is the case, then the criteria should presumably reflect that of these decision-makers. Yet it is far from clear that the typical decision-maker would even recognize the social welfare functions typically employed, still less accept them as embodying all their concerns. This becomes even more the case where the objectives are supposed to be those espoused by individual citizens (Atkinson 2011: 159, Chapter 15 in this volume).

If welfare economists were content to adapt their advice, as Samuelson suggests, to whatever interests a conceivable addressee may hold, be it a benevolent dictator, an egoist, a misanthrope, or whatever, they could surely count on finding attention if their advice is indeed instrumentally useful. Yet, this is surely not what welfare economics has traditionally been understood to be about. Being about *social welfare*, it has always been understood as providing advice on what serves the *common weal* of a community. Only for a welfare economics so understood is the question of whom it means to address of relevance. And it is in regard to its potential role in advising democratic politics that welfare economics has long been charged by public choice theorists of ignoring the incentives that participants in real world democratic processes are facing. Referring to Wicksell as precursor of public choice theory, Buchanan (1987: 243, Chapter 38 in this volume) states:

Stripped to its essentials, Wicksell's message was clear, elementary, and self-evident. Economists should cease proffering policy advice as if they were employed by a benevolent despot, and they should look at the structure within which political decisions are made.[261]

It is quite instructive that Ng in his textbook on welfare economics has the following to say on the public choice critique:

As in most studies in welfare economics, this book concentrates on analyzing what is socially optimal in some sense, as though presuming that governments will pursue social optimality. Over eighty years ago, Wicksell (1896) admonished economists for their failure to recognize the fact that governments don't behave like a benevolent despot. Collective decisions are undertaken by ordinary people like voters, politicians, and bureaucrats who usually base their decisions more on their own interests. This point has been repeatedly emphasized by Buchanan ... Despite substantial work in this area ... the impact upon orthodox economic writings has been small. This is partly due to the complicated nature of actual public choice processes and partly due to the fact that the simple social optimality approach can still usefully serve as an ideal to aim at, a standard to compare with, and a foundation to base further analysis on (Ng 1979: 281f.).

As the addressee issue that plagues welfare economics resurfaces in quite similar form in social choice theory, a few comments may suffice here. Arrow describes his view on the issue by contrasting it with that expressed by Bergson in the above-quoted statements. To his supposition that he is only "expressing the intent of welfare economics generally," Bergson (1954: 242) adds the comment:

But some may be inclined nevertheless to a different conception ... According to this view, the problem is to counsel not citizens generally but public officials. Furthermore, the values to be taken as data are not those which would guide the official if he were a private citizen. The official is envisaged instead as more or less neutral ethically. His one aim in life is to implement the values of other citizens as given by some rule of collective decision making. Arrow's theorem apparently contributes to this sort of welfare economics (ibid.).

After quoting Bergson's views extensively, Arrow comments on the above-cited passage:

My interpretation of the social choice problem agrees fully with that given by Bergson ..., though, as can be seen, this is not the view that he himself endorses (Arrow 1969: 224, Chapter 20 in this volume).

Arrow does surely not mean to claim that the statement he endorses describes the actual motivation of politicians who, in real politics, compete for office. His interest apparently is in the purely theoretical exercise of deriving what would be advisable in a world in which doing what "collective rationality" demands is the overarching aim in politics, whether or not there are any addressees in the real world, be it political agents or citizens-principals, who would have an interest in pursuing this goal. It is worth quoting what Bergson has to say on Arrow's construction:

We have been considering the possibility that the welfare economist might counsel not citizens generally, as was assumed initially, but a public official. What of the further possibility that he counsel nobody in particular but the community as such? Is not Arrow's theorem more meaningful in this light? Writings on welfare economics might often be construed as being directed at counseling the "community as such," viewed as something above and beyond individuals. With its references to "rational behavior on the part of the community," and the like, Arrow's study is a case in point. But a moment's reflection makes clear that such a conception cannot be very meaningful. After all, even if one prefers to think of the community as an "organic entity," he must still concede that in the last analysis all decisions are made by individuals. If one does not counsel individuals, who is there to counsel? (Bergson 1954: 243).

The same objection that Bergson directs at Arrow is invited when Sen (1987: 382) defines the project of social choice theory as determining "social preferences" in the sense of judgments on whether "society is better off in state x than in state y" or "judgements of the well-being of the community" (ibid.: 383). As Sen (1999: 355) posits, for such judgments "we cannot rely" on voting systems, because they would not include the preferences of those who do not exercise their "voting right" (ibid.), and because, even "with the active involvement of every one in voting exercises, we cannot but be short of important information needed for welfare-economic evaluation" (ibid.). Since democratic politics must necessarily be based on voting systems through which citizens-members exercise their decision-making authority as ultimate sovereigns, it is difficult to see who in actual politics, be it citizens or political agents, might have an interest in the recommendations that a social choice theory, as defined by Sen, may produce.

It is in the research program of constitutional political economy that the question of who is the intended addressee of policy advice finds the most obvious and unambiguous answer. It is clearly implied in the outlook on politics it takes, an outlook that Buchanan describes in these words:

> In my vision of social order, individual persons are the basic component units, and "government" is simply that complex of institutions through which individuals make collective decisions, and through which they carry out collective as opposed to private activities. "Politics" is the activity of persons in the context of such institutions. ... In my vision, or my model, individual persons are the ultimate decision-makers, and if we want to discuss government decision processes we must analyze the behavior of individuals as they participate in these processes. We do not conceive government as some supra-individual decision-making agency, one that is separate and apart from the individual persons for whom choices are being made. In other terms, I stress the "by the people" leg of the Lincoln triad (Buchanan [1968] 2000: 4).[262]

The conclusion to be drawn from this outlook on democratic politics for the addressee issue is obvious:

> If individuals are considered the ultimate sovereigns, it follows directly that they are the *addressees* of all proposals and arguments concerning constitutional-institutional issues. Arguments that involve reliance on experts in certain areas of choice must be addressed to individuals, as sovereigns, and it is individuals' choice in deferring to experts-agents that legitimizes the potential role of the latter, not some external assessment of epistemic competence as such (Buchanan [1991] 1999: 288f.).

With its choice-individualist perspective a constitutional political economy that seeks to advise citizens on ways to realize mutual gains or, in other words, to advance their common interests, naturally focuses its attention on the institutional framework within which policy choices are made, rather than on the content of these choices per se.[263] It sees its primary task in assisting "individuals, as citizens who ultimately control their own social order, in their continuing search for those rules of the political game that will best serve their purposes, whatever these might be" (Buchanan 1987: 250, Chapter 38 in this volume).

Political agents who act within the "rules of the political game" will surely be interested in advice on how they can be successful in the competition for office, but they will hardly be willing to follow recommendations for how to advance citizens' common interests if doing so is in conflict with their immediate interest in gaining, or staying in, office. Constitutional political economists do not see their proper task in providing advice of the former kind, and they do not expect to be particularly effective in providing the latter kind of recommendations. They consider their efforts to be best invested in exploring the potential for reforms in the institutions of politics that promise to better align political agents' immediate interests with citizens' common interests. Or, as Buchanan (1993) has put it in an essay title, their principal interest is in finding answers to the question:

> *"How Can Constitutions Be Designed so that Politicians Who Seek to Serve 'Public Interest' Can Survive and Prosper?"*

Notes

1. Samuelson (1947: 203, Chapter 6 in this volume): "Beginning as it did in the writings of philosophers, theologists, pamphleteers, special pleaders, and reformers, economics has always been concerned with problems of public policy and welfare." – Arrow (1951: 923): "Prescriptions for economic policy have been an integral and, indeed, controlling part of the economists' activities since the days of Jean Bodin."
2. Myrdal ([1922] 1953: 6, Chapter 2 in this volume) speaks of the "disregard shown by this early generation of the classical economists for the problem of delineating the science of economics from politics."
3. Scitovsky (1951: 303, Chapter 7 in this volume): "In the days of the classical economists, the whole body of economics was 'political economy,' centered around the welfare problem." – Nutter (1968: 166, Chapter 36 in this volume): "Economics, a child of the Enlightenment, was born as moral philosophy of the science concerned with how to build the good society. ... Adam Smith gave concrete form to the vision of his age in the *Wealth of Nations*, ... the founding treatise of economics or, more properly, political economy."
4. Smith ([1776] 1981: 11) notes about "different theories of political economy": "Those theories have had a considerable influence, not only upon the opinions of men of learning, but upon the public conduct of princes and sovereign states."
5. Myrdal ([1922] 1953: 1, Chapter 2 in this volume): "The task of economic science is to observe and describe empirical social reality and to analyze and explain causal relationships between economic facts. ... But the proposition that one state of society, actual or imagined, is politically preferable to another can never be inferred from the results of scientific work."
6. Jevons ([1871] 1965) made these remarks in the preface to the second edition of his textbook where he also commented on the fact that he kept the "old troublesome" name "Political Economy" in the title instead of using "Economics": "Though employing the new name in the text, it was obviously undesirable to alter the title-page of the book" (ibid.: xv).
7. Backhouse and Medema (2009: 224): "For Alfred Marshall, the main supporter of the term 'economics,' this renaming of the subject was part of establishing economics as a

professional scientific field."

8. Robbins (1981: 7, Chapter 13 in this volume): "In its beginning the label Political Economy covered a mélange of objective analysis and applications involving value judgments. ... In the last hundred years, however, beginning conspicuously, perhaps, with Alfred and Mary Marshall's *Economics of Industry* (1879), ... the label *Political Economy* as implying judgments of value, of which we do not wish to be accused, has tended to drop out of use."

9. Myrdal ([1922] 1953: 191): "There is, on the other hand, wide agreement that economics ought to be 'practical.' How then can the results of economic inquiry be made to serve practical purposes."

10. Walras ([1877] 1984: 63, Chapter 1 in this volume): "The theory of industry is called *applied science* or *art*; the theory of institutions *moral science* or *ethics*."

11. In his 1922 discussion on *The Political Element in the Development of Economic Theory* G. Myrdal ([1922] 1953: 13, Chapter 2 in this volume) noted: "The general thesis that economic science, if it is to be scientific, should refrain from attempting to establish political norms, has been accepted by leading economists for about hundred years and is a commonplace to-day. But the full significance of this postulate is apparently not generally grasped and the political doctrines are still with us."

12. In discussions on the value-judgment problem confusion is often caused by a failure to clearly distinguish what this problem actually entails from other questions raised by the role of value judgments in the social sciences. The principle of value-free science concerns the statements scientists make about their subject matter. It requires that scientists abstain from inserting value judgments in what they claim to be able to say about their subject matter. As Hans Albert (1965: 189ff.) has pointed out, value judgments in this sense should clearly be distinguished from three other kinds of value judgments that inevitably play a role in the social sciences but do not interfere at all with the postulate of value-free science. Firstly, there are value judgments in the subject area, that is, value judgments held by the persons whose behavior social scientists study. Secondly, there are value judgments inevitably involved in a scientist's choice of research topics from the infinite number of potential subjects. That such choice is explicitly or implicitly based on value judgments (about significance, career-promoting prospects, etc.) does not in the least mean that statements about the chosen subject cannot be kept free of any value judgment. And, thirdly, there are the above-discussed hypothetical value judgments on which every applied science is based. As noted, as hypothetical normative criteria they provide the focus for applied analysis but do not in any way interfere with the postulate of value-free science.

13. The failure to make this distinction is the cause of ambiguities that notoriously plague discussions on the status of welfare economics, as illustrated by the following quotations: "Modern economic theory draws a sharp distinction between positive economics, which explains the working of the economic system, and welfare economics, which prescribes policy" (Scitovsky 1941: 77). – "Welfare economics is obviously very closely related to normative economics which is concerned with what ought to be done and more generally with economic policy" (Little 2002: 19). – "While there is no consensus, a majority of economists seem to regard welfare economics as a normative discipline" (Ng 1979: 6).

14. Archibald (1959: 320, Chapter 9 in this volume) appears to take this view when he

argues: "The position I advocate may be summarized. ... The theorems of welfare economics are thus theorems of positive economics; they are concerned with the relationship between given ends and available means. Thus welfare theorems do not differ from theorems about, e.g., how full employment may be achieved."

15. Sugden (1981: 2): "The point of all this is that an economist who refuses to think about value judgments at all is helpless in the face of the sheer volume of facts at his disposal; every way of summarizing these facts will seem equally arbitrary to him."

16. Albert (1986: 91): "*Political* economy can as a comparative analysis of social control systems perfectly get by without value judgments – though not without hypothetically presumed criteria" (my translation).

17. Buchanan ([1982] 2001: 41): "Science is about the 'is,' or the conjectural 'is,' not about the 'ought.' ... Why does science have ultimate 'social' value? ... By more or less natural presumption, 'science' is valued because it is precursory to its usefulness in control. Physics, as positive science, is antecedent to the miracle of modern technology."

18. Albert (1979: 27): "Applied science (technology, including social technology) can at best show *possible courses of action* and – with regard to the problem of social order – *possible kinds of institutional arrangements* and their *general mode of functioning*. If a science of legislation is possible at all, it must at least contain a social technology of this kind. Going back two hundred years, we find a book which at that time was looked upon as an important contribution to the science of legislation – Adam Smith's *Wealth of Nations*."

19. Harrod (1938: 394) calls this "the criterion that individuals should get what they prefer," a criterion on which he comments: "In appraising institutions and practices and making recommendations, the economist has this criterion in mind; it constitutes the standard of good and bad. ... The economist is entitled to his criterion of individual preference. The politician may then say to him, 'I am not so much interested in individuals getting what they prefer, as in the country being self- sufficient. What I want to know is how to achieve this'."

20. Arrow (1994: 1): "[T]he typical economist's argument today for government intervention ... rests on individualistic valuations."

21. The prevalence in economics of *normative individualism* as the criterion of evaluation in policy analysis mirrors the prevalence of *methodological individualism* as analytical precept in economics as an explanatory exercise. – As Arrow (1994: 1) notes: "It is a touchstone of accepted economics that all explanations must run in terms of individuals. ... The unwieldly adjective, 'methodological,' is needed to distinguish the concern of constructing positive theory from the normative and policy implications wrapped up in the term 'individualism'."

22. As Bentham ([1789] 1982: 11) famously put it: "Nature has placed mankind under the governance of two sovereign masters, *pain* and *pleasure*. It is for them alone to point out what we ought to do, as well as to determine what we shall do. On the one hand the standard of right and wrong, on the other hand the chain of causes and effects, are fastened to their throne." – While Bentham's attempted short-cut from "is" to "ought" must be rejected as a naturalistic fallacy, his utilitarian measuring rod for assessing government actions can easily be re-interpreted as a hypothetical normative premise in the sense explained above, that is, a premise on which an applied economics can be based

that pronounces hypothetical imperatives for what government should do *if* the effects on individuals' utilities are taken as the relevant measuring rod.

23. Quoted from Georgescu-Roegen (1971: 343). As Georgescu-Roegen (ibid.) adds: "The individual is thus reduced to a mere subscript of the ophelimity function $\Phi_i(x)$." – After having described how an individual's indifference curves may be represented, Pareto ([1911] 1955: 61) notes: "Thereafter, the individual may disappear, we do not need him any longer in order to determine economic equilibrium."

24. Hausman and McPherson (1996: 69): "Economists typically evaluate outcomes in only one way – in terms of individual welfare. ... Since the evaluation of outcomes rests exclusively on their consequences for individual welfare, the theory of individual welfare is crucial to normative economics." – Suzumura (2010: 607): "As a matter of fact, ... the standard approach in normative economics captures the value of consequences only through individual utilities, or more broadly individual welfares, experienced ... by individuals who constitute the society or economy." – What Hausman and McPherson as well as Suzumura call "normative economics" can, in the sense explained above, for our purposes be re-interpreted as "applied economics."

25. Buchanan (1960: 5f.): "In an individualistic society, collective choice must represent some composite of individual choices."

26. Myrdal ([1922] 1953: 8) speaks of the "objective social philosophy of utilitarianism, of which economic science was but one specific elaboration."

27. Myrdal ([1922] 1953: 17): "If the moral philosophy of the utilitarians still survives in a fairly systematic shape, it owes this to the loving care with which it has been preserved in economic theory."

28. Arrow ([1951] 1963: 24) speaks of "Benthamite social ethics and its latter-day descendant, welfare economics." – Baujard (2016: 611f.): "Utilitarianism ... may be considered as the genuine root of welfare economics."

29. Scitovsky (1951: 303, Chapter 7 in this volume): "Welfare economics is that part of the general body of economic theory which is concerned primarily with policy. ... Welfare economics supplies the economist – and the politician – with standards ... by which to appraise and on the basis of which to formulate policy. Hence, whenever the economist advocates a policy ... he makes a welfare proposition."

30. Albert (1967: 156): "These issues had since long been central problems of political economy, yet today they appear to be sourced out to a special field, the so-called welfare economics" (my translation).

31. Sen (1997: 19, Chapter 22 in this volume): "Traditional welfare economics has tended to be 'welfarist' in the sense of assessing the merits of social states of affairs as a function of individual tilities. Combined with 'consequentialism', this leads to the assessment of all social decisions (about actions, institutions, etc.) in terms of the values of the associated utilities."

32. According to Mishan (1960: 199), the "most widely shared" ethical judgment in welfare economics is "that the welfare of the community depends on the welfares of the individuals comprising it, and on nothing else." – Just, Hueth and Schmitz (2004: 3) refer to the premise that "the welfare status of society must be judged solely by the members of society" as "the *fundamental ethical postulate* of the principle of *individualism*." – Baujard (2016: 612) states in summarizing his review of "the evolution of welfare

economics": "The only noteworthy element of continuity and unity is that most contributions were then welfarist, that is to say that the only relevant information for social welfare or public decisions was individual utilities."

33. Samuelson (1968: vii) opens his Foreword to the 1968 edition of Graaff's book with the statement: "If somebody asks me what modern welfare economics is about, I always recommend to them Graaff's *Theoretical Welfare Economics*."

34. Graaff ([1963] 1968: 34): "The function describing a man's hypothetical choices can be called his *utility* function. It should be emphasized that it describes choices, and in no way seeks to *explain* them."

35. Such a definition can hardly turn welfare economics into a "behaviorist approach" as Graaff (ibid.: 35) claims when he notes: "the utility function is primarily an expository device enabling us to talk about indifference curves without abandoning a behaviorist approach to welfare."

36. Suzumura (2000: 1): "[T]he standard history of this discipline begins with Arthur Pigou's monumental treatise, *The Economics of Welfare* (1920), with good reasons. Suffice it to observe that it was Pigou's path-breaking work that gave its name to this branch of economic analysis."
    – Hicks (1975: 307): "[T]he 'official' history, of course, begins with Pigou, *The Economics of Welfare* (1920). For it was certainly Pigou who gave its name to the subject. If it existed before Pigou, it must than have been called something else."

37. Suzumura (2010: 609): "It was Pigou (1920) who synthesized the long Cambridge traditions of moral philosophy into what he christened the *Economics of Welfare*. The epistemological basis of Pigou's synthesis was Benthamite utilitarianism." The "Cambridge tradition" includes John Stuart Mill, Henry Sidgwick and Alfred Marshall.

38. An often quoted statement from the Preface to the first edition of *The Economics of Welfare* (1920: vii) is: "The complicated analysis which economists endeavor to carry through are not mere gymnastics. They are instruments for the bettering of human life."

39. Little (1957: 9): "*The Economics of Welfare* purported to be an objective study of the causes of satisfaction; but it was regarded by its author as an ethical study, although the transition from the one to the other was not, and could not, be analyzed."

40. Smith ([1776] 1981: 258): "The real wealth of the country, the annual produce of its land and labour." – Vining (1956: 14) comments on Smith's use of the term: "The 'greatness of its produce' was the basis upon which he proposed to judge the performance of these different systems of political economy. The expected average 'welfare' of the members of the society, i.e. per capita income, would be different depending upon the particular system adopted."

41. Radomysler (1946: 202f.): "The task of welfare economics is to study the causes of welfare; what would make men happier, and what not. ...Welfare, or happiness, however, is no simple thing. What our welfare economists consider is only one part ... The idea of 'economic welfare' as a part of 'general welfare', is a misleading conception; welfare is a harmonious whole." – Mishan (1960: 256): "[A] study of welfare which confines itself to the measurement of quantities of goods and their distribution is not only seriously limited, it is ... positively misleading. For the things on which happiness ultimately depends ... are outside its range: only the most obstinate pursuit of formalism would endeavor to bring them into relation to the measuring rod of money, and then to no

practical effect."

42. Samuelson (1968: vii): "By 1930 the ethical hedonism of Bentham, Sidgwick, Edgeworth, and Marshall came under heavy attack by Gunnar Myrdal and Lionel (now Lord) Robbins." – Samuelson (in Suzumura 2004: 5): "I think Lionel Robbins' essay in 1932 was not only important for my thinking, but was important for the whole profession. I cannot autobiographically relate the influence of Gunnar Myrdal's book." – Both Robbins and Myrdal had in fact criticized more generally the use of value-laden terms in economics that conceal as positive claims what in fact are value judgments. Myrdal ([1922] 1953: 192) speaks of the "perpetual game of hide and seek in economics [that] consists in concealing the norm in the concept." About the purpose of his study, Myrdal (ibid.: 13) states: "There are no values in the objective sense, only subjective valuations. These should be distinguished from perceptions of reality. This idea is the central point of view of the present critical analysis of economic theory." – Robbins (1932: 129, Chapter 3 in this volume) notes as an example that in this regard "the use of the adjectives 'economical' and uneconomical' to describe certain policies is apt to be very misleading."

43. Samuelson (1981: 225): "The Old Welfare Economics … believed that cardinal utility was a scientifically definable magnitude for each person. With appropriate interpersonal constants these intrapersonal utilities could be added to form Total Social Utility, a magnitude that manifestly ought to be maximized." – Sen (1995: 3, Chapter 21 in this volume): "The subject of welfare economics was dominated for a long time by the utilitarian tradition, which performs interpersonal aggregation through the device of looking at the sum-total of the utilities of all the people involved."

44. Suzumura (2000: 3) notes about Pigou's definition: "This definition presupposes that the satisfaction or welfare of different individuals can be added to, or subtracted from, one another." – Little (1957: 8): "Professor Pigou himself took over the whole Benthamite doctrine that the welfare of society was the sum total of the welfares of the individuals, and that the welfare of an individual was the sum total of the satisfaction he experienced."

45. Bentham had specified in some detail how the "interest of the community" as the "sum of the interests of the several members who compose it" ([1789] 1982: 12, Chapter 4 in this volume) ought to be calculated (see ibid.: 39f.). As a caution he added: "It is not to be expected that this process should be strictly pursued previously to every moral judgment, or to every legislative or judicial operation. It may, however, be always kept in view and as near as the process actually pursued on these occasions approaches to it, so near will such process approach to the character of an exact one" (ibid.: 40).

46. Robbins (1981: 5, Chapter 13 in this volume) adds: "Of course, I do not deny that, in everyday life, we do make comparisons between the satisfactions of different people. … But these are *our* estimates. There is no objective measurement conceivable."

47. As regards the first of the above two quotations, the claim that satisfaction or utility can be compared across persons is clearly different from a claim such as that "A's preference stands above B's in order or importance." The latter is indeed a *value judgment* while the former is a *factual* claim that may be right or wrong, but is not per se "outside of positive science." – The same ambiguity is present in Robbins' (1938: 640) statement: "But I still think, when I make interpersonal comparisons (as, for instance, when I am deciding between claims affecting the satisfaction of two very spirited children), that my judgments are more like judgments of values than judgments of verifiable fact."

48. This postulate Robbins states in these terms: "Economics deals with ascertainable facts; ethics with valuations and obligations. The two fields of enquiry are not on the same plane of discourse. Between the generalizations of positive and normative studies, there is a logical gulf fixed which no ingenuity can disguise and no juxtaposition in space or time bridge over. ... Propositions involving the verb 'ought' are different in kind from propositions involving the verb 'is'" (Robbins 1932: 132f., Chapter 3 in this volume).

49. The noted ambiguity is also implied when Robbins (1932: 125, Chapter 3 in this volume) comments on the concept of "social utility": "Interesting as a development of an ethical postulate, it does not at all follow from the positive assumptions of pure theory. It is simply the accidental deposit of the historical association of English Economics with Utilitarianism: and both, the utilitarian postulates from which it derives and the analytical Economics with which it has been associated will be the better and the more convincing for the separation."

50. Robbins (1932: 126, Chapter 3 in this volume): "And suppose that ... we had succeeded in showing that certain policies *had the effect* of increasing 'social utility', even so it would be totally illegitimate to argue that such a conclusion by itself warranted the inference that these policies *ought* to be carried out. For such inference would beg the whole question whether the increase of satisfaction in this sense was socially obligatory."

51. Mishan (1980: 703): "Robbins once stood rightly insisting that the economist had no scientific means of checking his judgments about interpersonal comparisons of utility and, therefore, that policy recommendations founded on such assumed comparisons lacked scientific status." – In reacting to Robbins' charge, Pigou (1951: 292) has noted: "The issue for Welfare Economics is important. For, if the satisfaction of different individuals cannot be compared, a large part of that subject is undermined. ... To ask whether inter-personal comparisons of satisfactions or utilities are in fact possible is thus not an idle question."

52. Harsanyi (1969: 59) has pointed to the need to separate in Robbins' critique the factual issue of whether utilities can be interpersonally compared from the issue of normative judgments associated with such comparisons. – On the issue, Ng (1979: 5) comments: "[W]hile the problem of interpersonal comparability of utility is a tricky one, it is not insoluble in principle. It is conceivable that, perhaps several thousand (or million) years from now, neurology may have advanced to a stage where the level of happiness can be accurately correlated to some cerebral reaction which can be measured by a 'eudaimonometer'. ...The question whether we ought to pursue or maximize social welfare as objectively defined ... [based on such measurements] is however a value question."

53. Little (1957: 14): "[I]t has been held that the satisfaction and happiness of different people cannot be compared in an objective scientific way, and that any such comparison is a value, or an ethical judgment, and not an ordinary empirical judgment about a matter of fact." – Graaff ([1963] 1968: 167): "I have consistently referred to interpersonal comparisons of well-being as questions of ethics rather than questions of fact." – That the ambiguities about the status of the propositions of welfare economics persist is illustrated by Atkinson's remarks on "The Restauration of Welfare Economics": "Robbins is clearly right, in my view, in asserting that there are two different reasons why economists may disagree. We may disagree about the way in which we believe that the economy works;

or we may disagree about the criteria to be applied in judging economic performance. ... Where I part company from Robbins is that I believe that questioning the welfare criteria is a legitimate part of economics. ... Economics is a moral science. Welfare economics should be a central part of the discipline. ... Welfare economics has largely disappeared from sight, a disappearance that is strange in the sense that economists have not ceased to make welfare statements. ... Just taking the first 15 of the 46 articles in the 2006 *Economic Journal*, ... These articles are reaching clear normative conclusions ... There is, moreover, a public demand for such normative statements. ... [W]e cannot talk about *the* welfare consequences: there are several welfare criteria that could be applied in evaluating a change or a policy proposal" (Atkinson 2009: 791, 792, 793, 803).

54. See also Robbins' (1932: 133, Chapter 3 in this volume) remark: "Applied Economics consists of propositions of the form, 'If you want to do this, then you must do that'."

55. Hicks (1975: 308): "Thanks, in the main, to the work of Robbins and of Myrdal, Pigou's adherents were nearly confined to a narrow circle in his own university. The first phase was over; but there was a second phase to begin." – Little (2002: 11): "Doubtless influenced to some extent by Robbins, economists gave up the idea of cardinal utility." – Sen (1999: 352): "Thus, the epistemic foundations of utilitarian welfare economics were seen as incurably defective."

56. Scitovsky (1951: 303, Chapter 7 in this volume): "The ordinal nature of utility and the impossibility of interpersonal utility comparisons soon became axioms generally accepted by most people who were concerned with such matters." – Little (1957: 13): "The result of this criticism has been the general acceptance of a theory based on the view that only the ordinal number system, and not the cardinal number system, may be applied to satisfaction."

57. Harrod made it the central point of his argument that in order to be able to judge, for example in the case of the Repeal of the Corn Laws, its welfare consequences, all that was needed was "some sort of assumption about the equality of men in regard to their needs" (1938: 396), allowing one, for instance, to conclude that a difference of "two pence has lower utility to a millionaire than to a £25-p.-a. man" (ibid.). He emphatically stated: "No; some sort of postulate of equality has to be assumed" (ibid.: 397). – Responding to Harrod's objection Robbins noted: "Would it not be better, I asked myself, quite frankly to acknowledge that the postulate of equal capacity for satisfaction came from outside, that it rested upon ethical principle rather than upon scientific demonstration, that it was not a judgment of fact in the scientific sense, but rather a judgment of value ... In the realm of action, at any rate, the real difference of opinion is ... between those who hold that human beings should be treated as if they were equal and those who hold that they should not" (Robbins 1938: 637, 641). – In retrospect Robbins (1981: 7, Chapter 13 in this volume) commented on this issue: "I personally do not judge that, in any scientific sense, people are necessarily equally capable of satisfaction – whatever that may mean. I readily agree that personal entitlement in equal situations to equal treatment by law is desirable; and I would go beyond that in saying that, in personal relationships the treatment of one's fellows on the basis of equality answers my criterion of civilized behavior."

58. Baumol and Frish quote, in their own translation, similar passages from Pareto's 1906 *Manuale Di Economia Politica*:

Consider any position whatsoever, and suppose there is a very small departure from it, consistent with the circumstances of the case. If, as a result, the wellbeing of everybody in the group is augmented, it is evident that the new position is preferable to everyone in the group, and vice versa, it is undesirable if the wellbeing of everyone is diminished. The wellbeing of some may, moreover, remain constant without affecting our conclusions. ... It is these considerations which lead us to define a position as representing one of maximum ophelimity if it is such that it is impossible to depart from it by a small quantity in such a manner that all the ophelimity enjoyed by the individuals concerned increases or remains constant (Baumol 1946: 45).

Let us begin by defining a term which is very convenient to use in order to save words. We shall say that the individuals of a group in a given position have *maximum ophelimity* if it is impossible to depart some small distance from this position in such a way that this departure is useful for all the individuals of the group. Every small displacement from this position would necessarily have the effect of being useful to some of the individuals of the society and detrimental to some others (Frisch 1959: 91).

59. Buchanan (1959: 125, Chapter 10 in this volume): "The Pareto rule is itself an ethical proposition, a value statement, but it is one which requires a minimum of premises and one which should command wide assent." – Mishan (1980: 702): "[A]doption of a potential Pareto improvement as an economic criterion has also to rest on a value judgment; more precisely, on the economist's belief that such a criterion would command an ethical consensus."

60. Samuelson (1981: 224) credits Little with having coined this term.

61. Myrdal ([1922] 1953: 191): "We can ... safely say that, whenever interest harmony prevails, economists can make universally valid recommendations." – While policy recommendations based on the Pareto criterion are surely uncontroversial among economists who accept, explicitly or implicitly, a *normative individualism*, they are not necessarily uncontroversial for someone who believes in a theocratic or Marxist-Leninist approach to politics.

62. The paradigmatic difference between utility-individualism and choice-individualism is also obscured when Graaff ([1963] 1968: 7) states: "It would be very convenient if we could define group welfare in exactly the same way as individual welfare ... Unfortunately, however, groups do not frequently make unanimous choices. Majorities, it is true, often agree; but we are interested in the welfare of the whole group, not just the majority."

63. Sen (1999: 352): "This criterion takes no interest in *distributional* issues, which cannot be addressed without considering conflicts of interest and of preferences. Some *further* criterion is clearly needed for making social welfare judgements with a greater reach."

64. Scitovsky (1941: 79): "It would hardly be satisfactory, however, to confine the economist's value judgments to cases where one situation is superior to the other from the point of view of everybody affected. It is doubtful if in practice any choice comes within this category." – Van den Doel and Van Velthoven (1993: 32): "The practical objections to the Pareto criterion concern the problem that changes in social welfare which comply with the criterion do not often occur. Nearly every improvement of utility for some individuals is associated with a fall in utility for others."

65. Hicks (1975: 308): "It was at this point that a hint was discovered in one of the more obscure chapters of Pareto's Manual, which seemed for a while to provide a solution.

Pareto himself was the father of ordinalism ... Though he wrote before Pigou, he appeared, to the adherents of the 'New Welfare Economics' (as it came to be called), to have solved Pigou's difficulty." – Sen (1995: 3, Chapter 21 in this volume): "Because of the eschewal of interpersonal comparability of individual utilities, the 'new welfare economics' that emerged tried to rely only on one basic criterion of social improvement, the Pareto criterion."

66. Robbins (1981: 6, Chapter 13 in this volume) has pointed out that the compensation argument had been made before by Jacob Viner in reference to the issue of international trade. – Viner (1937: 533f.) had argued "that free trade ... necessarily makes *available* to the community *as a whole* a greater physical real income in the form of more of *all* commodities, and that the state, if it chooses, can, by appropriate supplementary legislation, make certain that the removal of duties shall result in more of *every* commodity for *every* class of the community." For instance, Viner (ibid.: 534) notes, by "levying *internal* taxes" on goods more readily available by the removal of import duties, the state could use the proceeds to "offset an undesired effect of the reduction of duties on the distribution of the national income."

67. Scitovsky (1941: 79) argued that the compensation test is "not independent of value judgments between alternative income distributions" and that it may produce inconsistent results when one compares the "satisfaction yielded by the physical income" in the original and in the new situation with what it would be if the physical product were distributed as it was in the respective alternative situation. With such comparison, Scitovsky showed, there are instances when the compensation test may speak for adopting a particular reform as well as for reversing it. – On the "Scitovsky paradox" see for example Baumol (1946: 46); Mishan (1960: 220, 254); Kleinewefers (2008: 46).

68. Kaldor (1939: 551, fn. 1) acknowledges: "An increase in the money value of the national income (given prices) is not, however, necessarily a sufficient indication of this condition being fulfilled: for individuals might, as a result of a certain political action, sustain losses of a non-pecuniary kind."

69. Robbins (1981: 7, Chapter 13 in this volume) notes on the practicality of *actual* compensation: "But very little reflection is needed to raise doubts whether this is a sensible principle."

70. That general acceptance would be the relevant test of actual compensation Kaldor (1939: 551, fn.1) implies when he notes that in the case of policies allowing for compensation there would be "no interpersonal comparison of satisfaction involved ... because any such policy *could* be carried out in a way as to secure unanimous consent."

71. Baumol (1946: 46): "It turns out then that Mr. Kaldor's criterion in its most general sense has not eliminated the problem of interpersonal comparison of utility. It has only subjected utility to the measuring rod of money, a measuring rod which bends, stretches, and ultimately falls to pieces in our hands." – Little (1957: 93): "Thus all that needed to be proposed was that whenever one could say 'this would enable the gainers to overcompensate the losers' then one could also say 'this would increase general economic welfare'. The muddle between a sufficient criterion and a test has to a certain extent persisted, suggesting that some economists are still utilitarians at heart, and believe that the general welfare is some homogeneous kind of emotion which one can measure." – See also Kleinewefers (2008: 47).

72. Samuelson (1981: 225) speaks of the compensation school as "an approach that when stripped of its pretensions was revealed to merely catch up to the concept of Pareto optimality."

73. Chipman and Moore (1978: 581): "When all is said and done, the New Welfare Economics has succeeded in replacing the utilitarian smoke-screen by a still thicker, and more terrifying smoke- screen of its own."

74. Samuelson (1981: 225): "For a long time scholars confused two versions of the New Welfare Economics:

    1. The narrow version that emphasized and stopped short at 'compensation payments' made by gainers to losers (or determined to be *capable* of being made, *even if not actually made*.) ....
    2. Bergson's synthesis of the Old Welfare Economics of the additive-hedonistic type with the more general notion of a Social Welfare Function that introduces, from outside positivistic economic science, ethical norming of alternative states of the world. Within this broad genus, interest attaches to those species that involve ethics of individualistic type rather than of *paternalistic* type."

75. Samuelson (1968: vii): "Professor Bergson of Harvard, while still a young graduate student, founded in a too-little known article in the 1938 *Quarterly Journal of Economics*, the modern theory of welfare economics."

76. The original publication was under the name Abram Burk, Bergson's birth name. On the change of name see Samuelson (2004: 24).

77. Varian (1975: 23): "[T]he choice of a welfare function 'solves' the problem of choosing a best Pareto efficient point." – Graaff ([1963] 1968: 8f.): "[E]conomists do not really mean that interpersonal comparisons are 'impossible'. All that they mean is that they cannot be made without judgements of an essentially ethical nature. If we make these explicitly, we can formalize them in the shape of a Bergson social welfare function of the individualistic type. ... It either summarizes or implies a detailed set of ethical judgements regarding the way in which one man's welfare is to be 'added' to another's." In a footnote Graaff explains that the characterization as "individualistic type" means that the variables on which the function depends are "the individual utility indicators."

78. Samuelson (1968: vii): "Bergson was thus able to avoid (or, alternatively, to include) the hedonistic summation of cardinal utilities, and at the same time to value at their true (limited) worth the Pareto-optimality necessary conditions that are themselves expressible independently of a social welfare function. So to speak, this put the narrow 'new welfare economics' of Pareto, Hotelling, A.P. Lerner, Kaldor, and Hicks in its proper place." – Arrow ([1951] 1963: 108) notes in reference to the compensation school: "[T]his 'new welfare economics' says nothing about choices among Pareto-optimal alternatives. The purpose of the social welfare function was precisely to extend the unanimity quasi-ordering to a full social ordering."

79. Ng (1979: 3) comments on a "Paretian social welfare function" or "individualistic Bergson SWF": "A Paretian SWF accepts the Pareto criterion. ... But a change need not necessarily satisfy the Pareto criterion to be regarded as a good change according to a Paretian SWF. For example, a change may make a few individuals marginally worse off but many individuals significantly better off. It may be regarded as a good change by a

Paretian SWF."
80. Samuelson (2004: 23): "[M]y own work in welfare economics owes virtually everything to his classic 1938 *Quarterly Journal of Economics* article that for the first time clarified this subject."
81. Samuelson (1981: 228): "My *Foundations of Economic Analysis* treatment of welfare economics in Chapter 8 still reads as a convenient summary of the Bergsonian Weltanschauung. Jan von de Graaf's *Theoretical Welfare Economics* (1957) provides an elegant and useful treatment of the same subject." – Samuelson (1983: xxi): "Until that chapter was available, only those who knew Bergson's seminal 1938 *Quarterly Journal* article or Oscar Lange's 1942 *Econometrica* article could find their way through the swamp of assertion, truth, ambiguity, denial, and misunderstanding that went under the name of the 'new welfare economics'."
82. Tintner (1946: 70) notes on Bergson's social welfare function: "This is equivalent to the assumption that now the community forms a judgment about the relative importance of the utility of all individuals."
83. On the "individualistic ethical requirement" Samuelson (1977: 85) comments, "that '... individuals' tastes are to "count" in the sense of being "respected" when all persons are in agreement on a move and are only to be supplemented for moves involving tradeoffs between different individuals, tradeoffs that can be resolved only by specified ethical norms or judgments'."
84. As far as the "individualistic" component of the social welfare function is concerned, it reflects a similar attitude of indifference when Samuelson (1967: 45) notes: "Now it is a 'natural' requirement in a culture obsessed by 'individualism' to require that the social ordering be somehow defined in terms of the specified individuals' orderings."
85. Scitovsky (1951: 311, Chapter 7 in this volume): "In fact, the social welfare function, as Bergson defines it, is so completely general that it is impossible to tell, on the basis of internal evidence alone, what use Bergson wanted to make of it. It may be that he aimed merely at a formal and rigorous restatement of the main problems of welfare economics." – Harsanyi (1969: 46) notes that Bergson proposed a "social welfare function, defined as an arbitrary mathematical function of economic (and other social) variables, of a form freely chosen according to one's personal ethical (or political) value judgments. Of course, in this terminology everybody will have a social welfare function of his own."
86. In reference to what Arrow calls the social welfare function's "second-order evaluation," Lange (1942: 219) speaks of "the subject exercising the valuation being an agency of the organized community," adding in a footnote: "In a democratically organized community these agencies will have to reflect the valuations of the majority." – Tintner (1946: 72) comments on the same issue: "[A] socialist government will attach large social significance to the workers, who favor public ownership, and low significance to the middle class, which does not. The opposite might be true for a government devoted to laissez-faire liberalism. ... [A] socialist government may attach large social significance in publicly owned commodities use, e.g., by workers, and low significance to privately owned commodities, used, say, by capitalists. A laissez-faire government may make the opposite evaluations."
87. In this section all references without an author name are to Harsanyi's works.
88. Samuelson (2004: 26): "John Harsanyi restored some credence to the pre-Bergson

cardinality of the individual utilities and of Social Cardinal Utility."

89. Harsanyi (1969: 60): "[I]n welfare economics we have also found that a rational man (whose choices satisfy certain simple postulates of rationality and impartiality) must likewise act as if he made quantitative interpersonal comparisons of utility, even if his factual information is insufficient to do this on an objective basis."

90. Harsanyi (1969: 55): "There is no doubt about the fact that people do make, or at least attempt to make, interpersonal comparisons of utility, both in the sense of comparing different persons' total satisfaction and in the sense of comparing increments or decrements in different persons' satisfaction. The problem is only what logical basis, if any, there is for such comparisons.

   In general, we have two indicators of the utility that *other* people attach to different situations: their preferences as revealed by their actual choices, and their (verbal or nonverbal) expressions of satisfaction or dissatisfaction in each situation. But while the use of these indicators for comparing the utilities that a *given* person ascribes to different situations is relatively free of difficulty, their use for comparing the utility that different persons ascribe to each situation entails a special problem."

91. On the place of ethics within the "general theory of rational behavior," Harsanyi (1977a: 10) comments: "In contrast to individual decision theory, both game theory and ethics deal with rational behavior in a social setting. But *game theory* deals with individuals who rationally pursue their *own* self-interest ... against *other* individuals who just as rationally pursue *their* own self-interest
   ... On the other hand, *ethics* deals with a rational pursuit of the interests of *society* as a whole. The basic concept is that of *moral value judgments*."

92. Harsanyi (1977b: 50): "Thus under our model each individual i in effect has two different preference scales. The preferences expressed by his social welfare function W_i may be called his *moral* or *social preferences*, while those expressed by his utility function U_i may be called his *personal preferences*. By definition his actual choice behavior will be governed by his personal preferences, whereas his moral value judgments will be governed by his moral preferences. Accordingly only his personal preferences can be called his 'preferences' in the strict sense of the word. His moral preferences are only 'conditional preferences,' because they indicate merely what he *would* prefer *if* he gave equal weight to each individual's interests in choosing between alternative social situations."

93. Harsanyi (1977a: 10): "[T]he *arithmetic mean of all individuals' cardinal utility levels* in the society ... is the quantity that we are trying to maximize when we are making a moral value judgment." – Harsanyi (1998: 290): "As I tried to show in earlier publications ..., the impartially considered welfare of society as a whole at any given time can be measured by its social utility function, defined as the arithmetic mean of all individuals' utility functions in this society."

94. Harsanyi (1953: 434f.): "Now, a value judgment on the distribution of income would show the required impersonality to the highest degree if the person who made this judgment had to choose a particular income distribution in complete ignorance of what his own relative position (and the position of those near to his heart) would be within the system chosen." – Harsanyi (1977b: 49): "Individual *i*'s choice among alternative social situations would certainly satisfy this requirement of impartiality and impersonality, if he

simply *did not know in advance* what his own position would be in each social situation."

95. Harsanyi ([1977] 1982: 47): "My equiprobability model was first published in 1953, and was extended in 1955. ... Later John Rawls again independently proposed a very similar model, which he called the 'original position', based on the 'veil of ignorance'. But while my own model served as a basis for a utilitarian theory, Rawls derived very nonutilitarian conclusions from his own."

96. Harsanyi (1953: 435): "To sum up, the analysis of impersonal value judgment concerning social welfare seems to suggest a close affinity between the cardinal utility concept of welfare economics and the cardinal utility concept of the theory of choice involving risk."

97. See for example Harsanyi (1977b: 49f.).

98. Harsanyi (1953: 435): "This choice in that hypothetical case would be a clear instance of a 'choice involving risk.' Of course, in the real world value judgments concerning social welfare are usually not of this type, in that they do not presuppose actual ignorance of how a certain measure under discussion would affect one's personal interests; they only presuppose that this question is voluntarily disregarded for a moment."

99. See also for example Harsanyi (1958: 311f.): "The hypothetical impartially sympathetic observer must judge the consequences that a given action has for various people ... in terms of the attitudes, wants, desires, preferences of these people themselves. ... The value of pleasures, or higher mental states, or anything else, to any particular person he can judge ultimately only on the basis of the importance this person himself assigns to it."

100. Harsanyi (1969: 59): "On the other hand, if the information needed is available, individualistic ethics consistently requires the use, in the social welfare function, of individual utilities not subject to restrictive postulates. The imposition of restrictive ethical or political postulates on the individual utility functions would ... decrease the dependence of our social welfare function on the actual preferences ... of the individual members of society."

101. On the principle of preference autonomy, Harsanyi (1977b: 52) comments: "This is, of course, merely the familiar *principle of consumers' sovereignty*, often discussed in the literature of welfare economics. The interests of each individual must be defined fundamentally in terms of his own personal preferences and not in terms of what somebody else thinks is 'good' for him."

102. Sen (1997: 20, Chapter 22 in this volume): "Among the approaches that accept the central relevance of individual advantages for social decisions, there are those that dispute the preference-centered way of assessing individual advantage. There is, first of all, the issue of 'irrationalities', and also the presence of what Harsanyi (1955) calls 'antisocial' elements, which call for 'laundering' of preferences ... . The ethics of such 'purification' may be quite complex."

103. In addition to "irrational" preferences, Harsanyi (1988: 136, Chapter 14 in this volume) also counts "spurious," "malevolent" and "external" preferences among those that do not deserve to be respected in determining "social utility." – On this see also Harsanyi (1958: 312f.; 1988: 131ff., Chapter 14 in this volume).

104. Harsanyi (1977b: 64): "We do not always feel obliged to accept other people's utility functions uncritically but rather feel free to 'correct' them for factual errors and even to

'censor' them for antisocial attitudes."

105. Harsanyi (1977b: 64): "Thus our position may be called *critical rule utilitarianism*, as distinguished from ordinary rule utilitarianism, which would simply accept people's utility functions as they are, i.e., which would follow the principle of acceptance without any qualification."

106. Harsanyi is, though, somewhat ambiguous about the focus of his approach. While his declared primary concern is with rules and institutions, he also notes that his theory is about "alternative government policies, alternative patterns of income distributions, and so forth" (1977b: 49).

107. Harsanyi (1958: 313): "[T]he question of what is and what is not 'good' for other people should be judged ultimately in terms of their own 'preferences'."

108. Harsanyi (1958: 307): "Suppose I am told 'If you want to follow Christian ethics, do X', or ... 'If you want to gain the approval of an impartial and sympathetic observer, do X' – this will be a good reason for me to do X, provided that I do want to follow Christian ethics ... or to gain the approval of an impartial and sympathetic observer. These statements supply a good reason for doing X because they make an appeal to an attitude which I actually entertain and suggest a pattern of behavior corresponding to this attitude."

109. For a more detailed exposition of this argument see Vanberg ([1988] 1994 and 2008).

110. The monograph is an expanded version of Arrow (1950, Chapter 17 in this volume).

111. Sen (1997: 16, Chapter 22 in this volume): "Arrow was, in fact, in line with that remarkable group of French mathematicians, including Borda (1781) and Condorcet (1785), who had founded the discipline of democratic collective decisions in the 18th century, thereby extending the reach of European enlightenment to formal analysis of social aggregation and consensual governance. In several different ways, social choice theory is an inheritor of that post-enlightenment tradition, and the reliance on individual values in making social decisions is a part of that intellectual inheritance."

112. Sen (1999: 350): "The motivation that moved the early social choice theorists included the avoidance of both instability and arbitrariness in social choice. The ambition of their work focused on the development of a framework for rational and democratic decisions for a group, paying adequate attention to the preferences and interests of all its members. ... They noted, for example, that majority rule can be thoroughly inconsistent."

113. Arrow (1969: 228, Chapter 20 in this volume): "Now it has been known for a long time that the system of majority voting can give rise to paradoxical consequences. ... One might be tempted to suppose that the paradox of voting is an imperfection in the particular system of majority voting and more ingenious methods could avoid it. But unfortunately this is not so."

114. In this section references without an author name are to Arrow's works.

115. In retrospect Arrow has commented on his *Social Choice and Individual Values*: "This was at least asking some very fundamental questions about the whole nature of social intercourse and particularly about legitimation of collective action" (Arrow and Kelly 2010: 16).

116. Arrow (1987: 124): "Economic or any other social policy has consequences for the many diverse individuals who make up the society or economy. It has been long taken for granted in virtually all of economic policy discussion since the time of Adam Smith, if

not before, that *alternative policies should be judged on the basis of their consequences for individuals.*"

117. It sounds like a direct comment on Harsanyi's above-quoted arguments on "true preferences" when Arrow (1969: 219, Chapter 20 in this volume) states: "An observer looking from the outside on our isolate individual may say that his decision was wrong either in the sense that it was made on grounds of insufficient information or improper calculation. The latter possibility is a real and important one, but I will simply state that I am abstracting from it in the present discussion. The former interpretation I am rejecting here. For the single isolated individual there can be no other standard than his own values. He might indeed wish to change them under criticism, but this, I take it, means basically that he has not fully thought through or calculated the consequences of his actions and upon more consideration wishes to modify them."

118. Arrow ([1951] 1963: 4): "There has been controversy as to whether or not the economist *qua* economist could make statements saying that one social state is better than another."

119. Arrow ([1951] 1963: 22): "In Bergson's treatment, the tastes of individuals ... are represented by utility-functions, i.e., essentially by ordering relations; hence the Bergson social welfare function is also a rule for assigning to each set of individual orderings a social ordering of social states." – Commenting in retrospect on his original contribution, Arrow notes: "I dropped the U's which I never liked because I knew the U's were just disguises for R's for preference relations. I thought, while I was at it, I'd do an exposition starting from just the orderings" (Arrow and Kelly 2010: 4).

120. Arrow (1950: 335, Chapter 17 in this volume): "[T]he whole social ordering relation R is to be determined by the individual ordering relations for social states, $R_1, \ldots, R_n$."

121. Arrow (1963: 106): "All the writers from Bergson on agree on avoiding the notion of a social good not defined in terms of the values of individuals. But where Bergson seeks to locate social values in welfare judgments by individuals, I prefer to locate them in the actions taken by society through its rules for making social decisions. This position is a natural extension of the ordinalist view of values; just as it identifies values and choices for the individual, so I regard social values as meaning nothing more than social choices."

122. See also Arrow (1987: 124).

123. Sen (1987: 383): "Even though the focus has somewhat shifted in recent years from the impossibility results to other issues, there is no question at all that Arrow's formulation of the social choice problem in presenting his 'impossibility theorem' laid the foundations of social choice theory as it has evolved."

124. The theorem is presented in Arrow ([1951] 1963, 46–60). – See also Arrow (1987).

125. Arrow (1950: 336, Chapter 17 in this volume) comments on his theorem: "For simplicity of exposition it will be assumed that the society under study contains only two individuals and that the total number of alternatives which are conceivable is three. Since the results to be obtained are negative, the latter restriction is not a real one; if it turns out to be impossible to construct a social welfare function which will define a social ordering of three alternatives, it will a fortiori be impossible to define one which will order more alternatives. The restriction to two individuals may be more serious; it is conceivable that there may be suitable social welfare functions which can be defined for three individuals but not for two, for example. In fact, this is not so, and the results stated in this paper hold for any number of individuals. However, the proof will be considerably simplified by

considering only two."
126. On this controversy see e.g. Arrow (1958: 540; 1967: 48: 1977: 82; 1981: 228; 1983: xxii); Samuelson (1981: 228); Samuelson in Suzumura (2004: 15).
127. Emphasizing the "logical difference" between a Bergson–Samuelson social welfare function and Arrow's problem, Samuelson (1977: 82) notes that the latter is about how "different tastes and values of individuals are to be put into Arrow's Constitutional Voting-Machine Function for it to arrive at final decisions." – The analogy to a "voting machine" Little (1952: 427, Chapter 18 in this volume) had used when he commented on Arrow's approach: "Imagine the system as a machine which produces a card on which is written 'x is better than y,' or vice versa, when all individual answers to the question 'Is x better than y?' have been fed into it. ... Thus we can legitimately call the machine, or function, a decision-making process. But what would it mean to call the machine a social welfare function?"
128. Arrow (1969: 224, Chapter 20 in this volume): "The process of formation of welfare judgments is logically equivalent to a social decision process or constitution. Specifically, a constitution is a rule which associates to each possible set of individual orderings a social choice function, i.e., a rule for selecting a preferred action out of every possible environment. That a welfare judgment is a constitution indeed follows immediately from the assumption that welfare judgments can be formed given any set of individual preference systems for social actions. The classification of welfare judgments as constitutions is at this stage a tautology, but what makes it more than that is a specification of reasonable conditions to be imposed on constitutions, and it is here that any dispute must lie."
129. Arrow's "constitution" does not require the actual participation of the constituents as voters in the political process. Once their preference orderings are registered, they are no longer needed in order to make policy choices. Arrow ([1951] 1963: 30) speaks, in analogy to "the usual concept of consumer's sovereignty," of "citizens' sovereignty," but what he means by this term is that individuals' preferences are to count in the aggregation exercise, not that individuals' choices are to be respected. As he notes at the beginning of a section titled "The condition of citizens' sovereignty": "We certainly wish to assume that the individuals in our society be free to choose, by varying their values, among the alternatives available" (Arrow 1950: 338, Chapter 17 in this volume).
130. Arrow uses the term "collective decision making" in the ordinary sense, that is, the sense in which it cannot be meaningfully applied to market processes, when he speaks of "the need for normative and descriptive analysis of collective decision making" (1974b: 269), stating: "[T]here is an irreducible need for a social or collective choice on distribution. In point of fact, there are a great many other situations in which the replacement of market by collective decision making is necessary or at least desirable" (ibid.).
131. Farrell (1976: 9) refers to the ambiguous use of the term "social choice" when he notes: "However, it is open to Sen or Arrow to claim that they were using the term 'social choice' in an extended sense, so that the whole process leading to a social state is a social choice, no matter how unlike social choice the process may seem."
132. Sen (1987: 382): "Social choice theory, pioneered in its modern form by Arrow (1951), is concerned with the relation between individuals and society. In particular, it deals with the aggregation of individual interests, or judgments, or well-beings, into some aggregate

notion of social welfare, social judgment or social choice."

133. In this section all references without an author name are to Sen's works.

134. Suzumura (1996: 24): "Since the Pareto Principle has seldom been seriously challenged as a reasonable requirement on social welfare judgments, there is no wonder that Sen's impossibility theorem to the effect that *there exists no collective choice rule satisfying Sen's minimal liberty as well as the Pareto principle* causes a stir."

135. Sen (1983: 8): "A *social decision function* determines a complete and consistent (free from cycles) social preference defined over the set of alternative social states for any set (in fact, *n*-tuple) of individual preference orderings (one ordering per person). A social decision function has an *unrestricted domain* if it works for any logically possible n-tuple of individual preference orderings. The impossibility of the Paretian liberal is the theorem establishing that there cannot exist a social decision function satisfying unrestricted domain, the Pareto principle (even in its weak form), and minimal liberty ML."

136. On condition L Sen (1970: 153) comments: "The intention is to permit each individual the freedom to determine at least one social choice, for example, having his own walls pink rather than white, other things remaining the same for him and the rest of society." – In later publications Sen used such labels as "minimum liberty (ML)" for what he originally called the "condition of liberty (L)"; these terminological changes are not of relevance in the present context.

137. Sen (1997: 15, Chapter 22 in this volume): "Social choice theory is an analytical discipline which makes extensive use of axiomatic methods. Many of the strengths and weaknesses relate precisely to this analytical character, including the strength arising from its interpretational versatility and the weakness of a tendency towards formal neglect of substantive issues."

138. Rowley and Peacock (1975: 2): "Even Amartya Sen ... in our view remains confused as to the true nature of liberalism, which is not concerned, as he would have it, with the primacy of individual preferences, but rather with the maintenance and extension of individual freedom, defined as the absence of coercion of certain individuals by others."

139. Nozick (1974: 165f.): "The trouble stems from treating an individual's right to choose among alternatives as the right to determine the relative ordering of these alternatives within a social ranking. ... A more appropriate view of individual rights is as follows. Individual rights are co- possible; each person may exercise his rights as he chooses. The exercise of these rights fixes some features of the world."

140. On the traditional "control view of liberty" Sugden (1985: 216) comments: "The position to be formulated is that society ought to respect personal spheres. On the control view of liberty, this amounts to saying that individuals ought to be left free to make certain choices for themselves."

141. See also Sen (1979b: 552f.; 1983: 19f.; 1999: 363).

142. By "indirect liberty" Sen (1986: 232) means "that of people getting what they *would have chosen* even though they are not able to control all the decisions themselves."

143. Sen (1983: 18) nevertheless insists: "If we know that he has *not* got what he would choose, we know that his liberty has been violated, and that kind of deduction is all that is required for the impossibility of the Paretian liberal."

144. Sen (1983: 19): "When the outcome-evaluation interpretation of social preference is considered in the context of a purely procedure-based view of liberty, an outcome that is

regarded as 'better for society' from the point of view of liberty is so regarded precisely because that is what would be chosen by the person in question." – It is noteworthy that, in a joint paper with Williams, Sen appears to acknowledge the paradigmatic difference that he ignores in his impossibility theorem. Commenting on Harsanyi's concept of preference autonomy, Sen and Williams (1982: 13) argue there: "The derivation of importance of the thing chosen from the fact of choice must not be confused with the latter, but it belongs to an approach altogether different from utilitarianism, and is concerned with valuing the *capability to choose* rather than valuing *the thing chosen*. Valuing autonomy works directly in favor of supporting choice."

145. Sugden (1985: 225): "The procedures by which social decisions are made – or more accurately, by which individuals' choices combine to determine which social states come about – can be described by game forms. Then *a recognized personal sphere is a property of such a game form*, and is quite independent of individuals' preferences or hypothetical choices over social states."

146. Sen (1979a: 471): "[W]elfarism ... can be seen as imposing an 'informational constraint' in making moral judgments about alternative states of affairs." – Sen (2010: 36): "Welfarism, narrowly defined, is the demand that social welfare (or whatever is taken as the social maximand) depends only on individual utilities; other features of states of affairs have no direct influence on social welfare (or the social maximand)." – Sen (1979b: 548): "In its uncompromising rejection of the relevance of non-utility information welfarism is indeed a very limited approach."

147. Endorsing Sen's position, Suzumura (2000: 9) states: "The crucial feature of Arrow's social choice theory may be christened the *welfarist-consequentialism* ... where the assessment of consequences is exclusively in terms of people's welfare, their personal satisfaction, or people receiving what they want. Not only is Arrow's theory based on welfarist-consequentialism in this sense, but also it permeates through almost the entire edifice of traditional welfare economics, 'old' as well as 'new', and the contemporary social choice theory. It is this informational basis which, we contend, is to be held mainly responsible for the poverty of welfare economics."

148. Sen (1999: 365): "The possibility of constructive welfare economics and social choice (and their use in making social welfare judgments and in devising practical measures with normative significance) turns on the need for broadening the informational basis of such choice. Different types of informational enrichment have been considered in the literature. A crucial element in this broadening is the use of interpersonal comparisons of well-being and individual advantage."

149. One of Sen's claims is that with such removal of the informational restrictions the "impossibility problem" of Arrow's theorem disappears. See Sen (1979b: 539, 543; 1995: 8, Chapter 21 in this volume).

150. Without providing any detail, though, Sen (1999: 358) also claims that "even with such mental states comparisons, the case for unqualified rejection is hard to sustain," adding: "So the picture is not so pessimistic even in the old home ground of mental state comparisons. But, more importantly, interpersonal comparisons of personal welfare, or of individual advantage, need not be based only on comparisons of mental states."

151. In addition to allowing for nonutility information, Sen also wants the motivation behind persons' preferences to be considered in judgments on social choices. See Sen (1976:

219, 239; 1979a: 478, 482f.; 1979b: 550).

152. Sen (2010: 30): "[A]ll the social choice problems have the shared feature of relating 'social'- or group-assessments to the values, preferences, choices, or some other characteristic of the respective individuals who form the collectivity'."

153. In 1985 Buchanan published, jointly with Geoffrey Brennan, *The Reason of Rules*, subtitled *Constitutional Political Economy*, and in 1986 he used the name in his Nobel Prize lecture "The Constitution of Economic Policy" (Buchanan 1987: 250, Chapter 38 in this volume), the prize being awarded to him "for his development of the contractual and constitutional bases of economic and political decision-making."

154. References in this section without an author name are to Buchanan's works.

155. Buchanan (1990: 13): "For constitutional economics, the foundational position is summarized in *methodological individualism*. ... The autonomous individual is a *sine qua non* for any initiation of serious inquiry in the research program. Individual autonomy, as a defining quality, does not, however, imply that the individual chooses and acts as if he or she exists in isolation from and apart from the community or communities of other persons with whom he or she may be variously associated."

156. Buchanan (1990: 13): "[M]ethodological individualism, as a presupposition of inquiry, characterizes almost all research programs in economics and political science; constitutional economics does not depart from its more inclusive disciplinary basis in this respect."

157. Buchanan and Tullock (1962: vi): "The analysis [in this study] can perhaps be described by the term 'methodological individualism.' Human beings are conceived as the only ultimate choice makers in determining group as well as private action. Economists have explored in considerable detail the process of individual decision-making in what is somewhat erroneously called the 'market sector.' Modern social scientists have, by contrast, tended to neglect the individual decision-making that must be present in the formation of group action in the 'public sector'."

158. Buchanan and Tullock (1962: 13): "Collective action is viewed as the action of individuals when they choose to accomplish purposes collectively rather than individually, and the government is seen as nothing other than the set of processes, the machine, which allows such collective action to take place." – Buchanan (1962a: 308): "The State, or the polity, may be conceived as a set of rules or institutions through which individual human beings act collectively rather than individually or privately. That is to say, we may best describe what is normally called 'the State' in terms that specify such rules and institutions."

159. Buchanan (1959: 137, Chapter 10 in this volume): "Positive science is concerned with the discovery of 'what is,' normative science with 'what ought to be.' Positive economics, narrowly conceived, overly restricts the 'what is' category. Political economy has a non-normative role in discovering 'what is the structure of individual values.' The political economist, in accomplishing this task, can remain as free of personal values judgments as the positive economist."

160. Buchanan (1959: 128, Chapter 10 in this volume): "Propositions advanced by political economists must always be considered as tentative hypotheses offered as solutions to social problems." – Buchanan (1962a: 308): "We seek to learn how the social world works in order to make it work 'better,' to 'improve' things: this is as true for physical science as it is for social science."

161. Buchanan (1992: 152): "Critics have charged that my work has been driven by an underlying normative purpose. ... I shall acknowledge that I work always within a self-imposed constraint that some may choose to call a normative one. I have no interest in structures of social interaction that are non-individualist ... The individualist element in my vision of social reality, actual and potential, has been an important element in my substantive criticism of the work of others in political economy."

162. Arrow (2010: 26): "Social choice theory strips down the properties of the members to their preference scales." – Buchanan (1954: 119, Chapter 19 in this volume): "Arrow is primarily interested in individual values as the units of account to be used in deriving social welfare functions."

163. As Buchanan ([1991] 1999: 288) comments, "the normative premise of individuals as sovereigns" means that individuals "are the beings who are entitled to choose the organizational-institutional structure under which they live."

164. On the relation between an individual's preferences and his choices, Arrow (1969: 215f., 218f., Chapter 20 in this volume) notes: "One might ask him what action he *would choose* if offered some particular environment. By repeating this question for many alternative environments we have obtained a description of his values system in the sense of a rule giving his hypothetical choices for many or all possible environments. ... For the sake of economy of discussion we pass by many interesting issues. Most important, probably, is the relation between hypothetical choices and real ones. It is implied in the above discussion and below that a preference will in fact be translated into a choice if the opportunity ever comes. But the question may be raised how we can possibly know about hypothetical choices if they are not actually made. This is not merely a problem of finding out about somebody else's values; we may not know our own values until put to the crucial test." – On the same matter, Sen (1986: 217f.) states: "We can also distinguish between the problem of aggregating individual *interests* ... and that of aggregating individual judgments on some social matter .... Similarly, the individual preferences might be expressed by the persons themselves (e.g. by voting), or guessed by someone doing the aggregation exercise (e.g. by a Planning Commission arriving at a plan for the country by taking note of the interests of each group, or a person making a social welfare judgment by assessing what he sees to be the interests of different people)."

165. Buchanan (1959: 126, Chapter 10 in this volume): "Utility is measurable, ordinally or cardinally, only to the individual decision-maker. It is a *subjectively* quantifiable magnitude. While the economist may be able to make certain presumptions about 'utility' on the basis of observed facts about behavior, he must remain fundamentally ignorant concerning the actual ranking of alternatives until and unless that ranking is revealed by the overt action of the individual in choosing." – "Individual preferences, insofar as they enter the [welfare economist's] construction ... must be those which *appear to the observer* rather than those revealed by the behavior of the individuals themselves. In other words, even if the value judgments expressed in the function say that individual preferences are to count, these preferences must be those presumed by the observer rather than those revealed in behavior" (ibid.: 133).

166. In a textbook on *Welfare Economics* the author notes: "The technical problems of the existence of a utility function that represents an individual's preferences is discussed in Appendix 1B. In the text, we shall for the most part take the existence of a utility function

for granted" (Ng 1979: 15). – Graaff ([1963] 1968: 35) claims for his approach to welfare economics: "[T]he utility function is primarily an expository device enabling us to talk about indifference curves without abandoning a behaviorist approach to welfare. ... Assuming the existence of a utility function does not entail assuming the existence of any such thing or quantity as 'utility' or 'satisfaction'. Our definition of individual welfare still runs in terms of conjectural choices. But when economists were interested in explaining choices ... it seemed natural to suppose that a man would choose *A* rather than *B* if he anticipated greater satisfaction, or utility, from the former. Then 'preference' meant something more than 'conjectural choice'." – It reads like a comment on Graaff's argument when Buchanan (1959: 126, Chapter 10 in this volume) says about welfare economics: "The observing economist is considered able to 'read' individual preference functions. Thus, even though an 'increase in welfare' for an individual is defined as 'that which he chooses,' the economist can unambiguously distinguish an increase in welfare independent of individual behavior because he can accurately predict what the individual would, in fact, 'choose' if confronted with the alternative under consideration."

167. Buchanan (1987: 248, Chapter 38 in this volume): "One of the most exciting intellectual moments of my career was my 1948 discovery of Wicksell's unknown and untranslated dissertation *Finanztheoretische Untersuchungen* (1896), buried in the dusty stacks of Chicago's old Harper Library. ... Wicksell's new principles of justice in taxation gave me a tremendous surge of self- confidence. Wicksell, who was an established figure in the history of economic ideas, challenged the orthodoxy of public finance theory along lines that were congenial with my own developing stream of critical consciousness."

168. Buchanan ([1967] 1999: 287): "Wicksell suggested that the unanimous consent of all parties should be the criterion for decisions in fiscal matters. Although it was developed independently, it is evident that this criterion is the political counterpart of the Pareto criterion for optimality."

169. Van den Hauwe (1999: 612): "The Wicksellian criterion of efficiency focuses on subjective choice processes, in marked contrast to the Paretian optimality condition of neoclassical welfare economics, which permits an external observer to use individual utility as an objective measure of welfare. ... Efficiency is not a property of social states that could be specified or defined independently of the actions of individuals and the process of voluntary exchange."

170. Buchanan (1959: 127, Chapter 10 in this volume): "Given the assumption of ignorance, Paretian 'efficiency' cannot be employed in aiding a group in choosing from among a set of possible social policy changes. A specific change can be judged to be Pareto-optimal or 'efficient' only after it has, in fact, been proposed and the individual preferences for or against the change revealed." – Buchanan ([1988] 2001b: 140: "Wicksell's objective was to construct a criterion for efficiency in fiscal decisions, by which he meant the satisfaction of the demands of individuals as consumers of collectively financed goods and services, analogously to the satisfaction of consumer demands in the competitive market for private goods and services."

171. In retrospect Arrow has commented on his *Social Choice and Individual Values*: "This was at least asking some very fundamental questions about the whole nature of social intercourse and particularly about legitimation of collective action" (Arrow and Kelly 2010: 16).

172. As Buchanan ([1991] 1999: 288) puts it, according to "the normative premise of individuals as sovereigns ... the legitimacy of social or organizational structures is to be judged against the voluntary agreement of those who are to live or are living under the arrangements that are judged."

173. Buchanan ([1984] 1999: 270) refers to this distinction when he notes: "It is necessary to distinguish carefully between agreement or unanimity as a test for an 'efficiency-enhancing trade' and unanimity as a decision rule."

174. Hands (2013: 17, fn. 11) points to the need to keep separate the notion that "every individual is the best judge of his or her best interest" and the principle of "consumer sovereignty," stating: "The latter seems to mean that the consumer is free to choose, and the former seems to mean that what they choose is always in their best interest; these appear to be entirely different things."

175. Buchanan ([1985] 2001: 250): "Legitimacy can only be derived, at one level or another, from the voluntary consent of individuals." – Buchanan ([1991] 1999: 288): "The central premise of *individuals as sovereigns* does allow for delegation of decision-making authority to agents, so long as it remains understood that individuals remain as *principals*. The premise denies legitimacy to all social organizational arrangements that negate the role of individuals as either sovereigns or principals."

176. Buchanan and Tullock (1962: 94): "It may be quite rational for the individual to choose a majority voting rule for the operation of certain collectivized activities. Once this rule is chosen, collective decisions at the legislative or policy level will be made accordingly. However, under the operation of such a rule, the political economist, trying to advance hypotheses concerning the existence of 'mutual gains from trade' through the political process is severely restricted. ... [T]he political or welfare economist is left with no means of confirming or rejecting his hypothesis."

177. About the economist's outlook on markets as arenas for voluntary exchange, Buchanan ([1989] 1991: 37) says: "He or she does not evaluate the results of exchange teleologically against some previously defined and known scalar. Instead, he or she adjudges the exchange to have been utility enhancing for each trader to the extent that the *process* itself has embodied attributes of fairness and propriety. If there has been neither force nor fraud, and if the exchange has been voluntary on the part of both traders, it is classified to have been mutually beneficial."

178. Buchanan and Tullock (1962: 4): "In a genuine sense, economic theory ... provides us with an explanation of how separate individual interests are reconciled through the mechanism of trade or exchange."

179. Buchanan ([1983] 2000: 16): "The approach to economics that I have long urged ... was called catallactics, the science of exchange, by some 19th century proponents ... This approach to economics ... draws our attention directly to the *process* of exchange, trade, or agreement, to contract." – In a similar spirit F.A. Hayek (1976: 108) has criticized the usual practice of calling the market order an "economy." Because this term is, Hayek argues, derived from the Greek word for a household economy, it misleadingly likens the market to a deliberately organized enterprise. He states: "Since the name 'catallactics' has long been suggested for the science which deals with the market order ... it would seem appropriate to adopt a corresponding term for the market order itself. The term 'catallactics' was derived from the Greek verb *katallatein* (or *katallassein*) which meant,

significantly, not only 'to exchange' but also 'to admit into the community' and 'to change from enemy into friend'. ... From this we can form the English term *catallaxy* which we shall use to describe the mutual adjustment of many individual economies in a market."

180. Buchanan ([1977] 2001: 112): "To the extent that results can be fitted into the exchange pattern, economists can infer that *all* parties secure gains, as these gains are measured in terms of the participants' preferences and not those of the observer. ... This explanatory-evaluative task for the economist may be extended from the simplest to the most complex institutional structures." – Buchanan and Tullock (1962: 266): "We view collective decision-making (collective action) as a form of human activity through which mutual gains are made possible. Thus, in our conception, collective activity, like market activity, is a genuinely cooperative endeavor in which *all* parties, conceptually, stand to gain."

181. In retrospect Buchanan ([1989] 1999: 31) has noted about his 1963 presidential address: "My argument was that economics, as a social science, is or should be about trade, exchange, and the many and varied institutional forms that implement and facilitate trade, including all the complexities of modern contracts as well as the whole realm of collective agreements on the constitutional rules of political society."

182. Buchanan and Tullock (1962: 19): "Both the economic and the political relation represent cooperation on the part of two or more individuals. The market and the State are both devices through which cooperation is organized and made possible. Men cooperate through exchange of goods and services in organized markets, and such cooperation implies mutual gain. ... At base, political or collective action under the individualistic view of the State is much the same. Two or more individuals find it mutually advantageous to join forces to accomplish certain common purposes."

183. Buchanan (1990: 12): "In agreeing to be governed, explicitly or implicitly, the individual exchanges his own liberty with others who similarly give up liberty in exchange for the benefits offered by a regime characterized by behavioral limits."

184. Buchanan and Tullock (1962: 252): "The 'social contract' is, of course, vastly more complex than market exchange, involving as it does many individuals simultaneously. Nevertheless, the central notion of mutuality of gain may be carried over to the political relationship."

185. Buchanan (1964: 220, Chapter 26 in this volume): "[T]he approach to economics that I am advancing extends to cover the emergence of a political constitution. At the conceptual level, this can be brought under the framework of a voluntaristic exchange process. The contract theory of the state, as well as most of the writing in this tradition, represents the sort of approach to human activity that I think modern economics should be taking."

186. Buchanan and Tullock (1962: 250f.): "Insofar as participation in the organization of a community, a State is mutually advantageous to *all* parties, the formation of a 'social contract' on the basis of unanimous agreement becomes possible. Moreover, the only test of the mutuality of advantage is the measure of agreement reached. ... The early theorists (Hobbes, Althusius, Locke, and Rousseau) did assume consensus in the formation of the original contract. They did so because the essence of any contractual arrangement is *voluntary* participation, and no rational being will voluntarily agree to something which yields him, in net terms, expected damage or harm."

187. Buchanan (1987: 249, Chapter 38 in this volume): "[T]he research program of political

economy merges into that of contractarian political philosophy, both in its classical and modern variations. In particular, my own approach has affinities with the familiar construction of John Rawls."

188. Buchanan ([1972] 2001: 353): "When I first encountered John Rawls' conception of 'justice as fairness,' I was wholly sympathetic. ... Now that the book has appeared, I find myself less sympathetic with Rawls than I might have anticipated from my earlier reading of his basic papers."

189. Rawls (2001: 7): "Since in a democratic society citizens are regarded from the point of view of the political conception as free and equal persons, the principles of a democratic conception of justice may be viewed as specifying the fair terms of cooperation between citizens so conceived."

190. Buchanan (1962a: 318): "Both, the contractarians and their critics have been too much concerned with the origins of government. ... The relevance of the contract theory must lie, however, not in its explanation of the origin of government, but in its potential aid in perfecting existing institutions of government."

191. Rawls (1971: 14f.): "I shall maintain that the persons in the initial situation would choose two rather different principles: the first requires equality in the assignment of basic rights and duties, while the second holds that social and economic inequalities, for example inequalities of wealth and authority, are just only if they result in compensating benefits for everyone, and in particular for the least advantaged members of society."

192. Rawls comments on the "original position": "Conceptions of justice are to be ranked by their acceptability to persons so circumstanced. Understood in this way the question of justification is settled by working out a problem of deliberation: we have to ascertain which principles it would be rational to adopt given the contractual situation. This connects the theory of justice with the theory of rational choice."

193. The notion of such a "*contract*," concluded among identical persons behind a veil of ignorance, is in contrast with how Rawls defines a contract when he notes that the principles of justice "apply to the relations among several persons" and states that the "word 'contract' suggests this plurality" (1971: 16). – With the concept of an "overlapping consensus" that he uses in later writings, Rawls ([1985] 1999: 390) indicates that a *contract* among a plurality of persons is limited to the area of issues where their interests coincide.

194. Arrow (1973: 250) has commented on this difference between Rawls and Harsanyi, siding with the latter. Rawls (1971: 15) argues, "contrary to utilitarianism," that "a rational man would not accept a basic structure merely because it maximized the algebraic sum of advantages irrespective of its permanent effects on his own basic rights and interests." – One may ask what expectations, according to Rawls, a rational person is supposed to form behind a veil of ignorance concerning the "effects on his own basic rights and interests."

195. Buchanan (1979: 281): "The behavioral paradigm in economics is that of the trader whose Smithean propensity to truck and barter locates and creates opportunities for mutual gains. This paradigm is contrasted with that of the maximizing engineer who allocates scarce resources among alternatives."

196. Buchanan ([1975] 2001: 79): "Where did economics, as a discipline, take the wrong turn? My own suggestion is that Lionel Robbins marks a turning point. His book defined

'the economic problem' as the location of maxima and minima." – Buchanan (1964: 214, Chapter 26 in this volume): "[Robbins'] all too-persuasive delineation of our subject field has served to retard, rather than to advance, scientific progress."

197. Frisch (1959: 39) illustrates such "natural extension" when he notes: "The purpose of a macro- economic decision model is to discuss which economic policy might be designated as 'good' or perhaps as 'the best' under given circumstances. ... The discussion of the general problem may ... take as its starting point a theoretical device for describing the preferences of any economic entity, whether a person, a family, a business enterprise, a public authority, etc. Such a device is the *preference function* of that entity. For shortness such an entity will be referred to as an 'individual'. In other words, we assume that each individual acts *as if* there exists a function which this individual tries to maximize."

198. Rawls (1971: 27): "In each case there is a single person whose system of desires determines the best allocation of limited means."

199. Myrdal ([1922] 1953: 17, Chapter 2 in this volume): "The idea that the economic process represents the economy of a personified society which tries to make the best of the available resources, thus working towards a common goal, remained the generally accepted form of reasoning in economics and governed the formulation and proof of its political doctrines."

200. Albert (1967: 159f.): "As Myrdal has shown, the arguments of welfare economics are based on the 'communistic fiction' of ... an economy ... as a collective subject. ... Ignoring all conflicts of interest, the idea of rational action, of action according to the economic principle, is projected to society as a whole" (my translation). – Albert (1998: 3) credits Myrdal for having exposed "the contradiction between the *individualistic presuppositions* of economic thought and the *communistic fiction* that one finds when it comes to matters of valuation" (my translation).

201. Arrow (1974a: 16): "An economist by training thinks of himself as the guardian of rationality, the ascriber of rationality to others, and the prescriber of rationality to the social world. ... From the economist's point of view ... collective action can extend the domain of individual rationality."

202. Buchanan ([1978] 2000: 45): "Since political outcomes emerge from a process in which many persons participate rather than from some mysterious group mind, why would anyone have ever expected 'social welfare functions' to be internally consistent."

203. On economists who extend the maximization paradigm to "the community or collectivity as a unit," Buchanan ([1979] 1999: 256) comments: "To those economists who made such an extension, Arrow's impossibility theorem was a genuinely shocking revelation. A 'social welfare function' must be constructed to allow for some modeling of the collectivity in teleological terms, but such a function becomes a logical impossibility under plausible conditions. What to do? What to do? I need not say that the welfare economists, among whom I should surely include Kenneth Arrow himself, are, to this day, groping for answers."

204. Buchanan and Tullock (1962: 32): "Under the individualistic postulates, group decisions represent the outcome of certain agreed-on rules for choice after the separate individual choices are fed into the process. There seems to be no reason why we should expect these final outcomes to exhibit any sense of order which might ... be said to reflect rational social action."

205. Referring to the Nobel Prize lecture (Arrow 1974b), in which "Arrow continues to hold that 'the philosophical and distributive implications of the paradox of social choice are still not clear'," Buchanan ([1975] 2001: 84) states: "The statement is both surprising and personally disappointing, since it indicates that Arrow has paid no heed to the arguments which I have made, along with many others, against the whole notion of collective rationality."

206. Van den Doel and Van Velthoven (1993: 89): "Thus, unanimity in political decision-making only has meaning as an ideal ... It is totally useless as a practical norm."

207. Buchanan (1987: 249, Chapter 38 in this volume): "Because of his failure to shift his own analytical construction to the level of constitutional choice, Wicksell was confined to evaluation of the political process in generating current allocative decisions. ... Distributional questions remain outside of the Wicksellian evaluative exercise ... With the shift to the constitutional stage of politics, however, this constraint is at least partially removed."

208. Wicksell ([1896] 1958: 89f., Chapter 24 in this volume): "Provided the expenditure in question holds out any prospect at all of creating utility exceeding costs, it will always be theoretically possible, and approximately so in practice, to find a distribution of costs such that all parties regard the expenditure as beneficial and therefore approve it unanimously."

209. Buchanan ([1968] 1999: 146f.): "Wicksell's contribution provides an indispensable groundwork for any further examination of political institutions or rules. It is necessary, however, to go beyond these simple efficiency limits, since even casual observation reveals that seldom, if ever, are unanimity rules (or even rules for relative unanimity) written into actual political constitutions. Experience surely suggests that efficiency in making group or collective decisions may necessarily involve departures from the restrictive Wicksellian limits, which would require that each single group choice be Pareto-Wicksell efficient."

210. Buchanan (1987: 248, Chapter 38 in this volume): "[A]n individual may rationally prefer a rule that will, on particular occasions, operate to produce results that are opposed to his own interests. The individual will do so if he predicts that, on balance over the whole sequence of 'plays,' his own interests will be more effectively served than by the more restrictive application of the Wicksellian requirement in-period."

211. Buchanan and Tullock (1962: 93): "When it is recognized that resources must be used up in the process of reaching decisions and that these genuine-resource costs increase rapidly as the decision- making unit is expanded to include more members of the group, it is relatively easy to see that the rational individual will deliberately choose ... rules that require less-than-unanimous consent of all members to decisions." – Buchanan (1990: 9): "Generalized agreement on constitutional rules that allow for the reaching of ordinary collective decisions by means that do not require general agreement is surely possible, as is empirically demonstrated in the context of almost all organizations."

212. Buchanan ([1978] 2000: 46): "Uncertainty about just where one's own interests will lie in a sequence of plays or rounds of play will lead a rational person, from his own interest, to prefer rules or arrangements or constitutions that will seem to be 'fair', no matter what final positions he might occupy." – There are obvious similarities between the "veil of uncertainty" in Buchanan and Tullock's theory of constitutional choice and the "veil of

ignorance" in Rawls' theory of justice. The important difference is that Rawls' veil is a purely hypothetical construct while Buchanan and Tullock's veil is a factual attribute of any choice of "rules of the game" with the "thickness" of the veil varying from case to case. – See Vanberg and Buchanan (1989: 52ff.).

213. Nutter (1968: 169, Chapter 36 in this volume): "[T]he problem of welfare economics is essentially the problem of choosing and implementing social policies. The first task is ... to choose the economic system. I would argue that this is the foremost task, to which all others are quite subservient. Viewed in this context, the fundamental problem is not one of making the rules to guide social activities, but rather one of making rules for making rules. The constitution comes first, and then specific laws and policies."

214. Buchanan and Tullock (1962: 96): "The individualistic theory of the constitution that we have been able to develop assigns a central place to a single decision-making rule – that of general consensus or unanimity. The other possible rules for choice-making are introduced as variants from the unanimity rule. These variants will be rationally chosen not because they will produce 'better' collective decisions (they will not), but rather because, on balance, the sheer weight of the costs involved in reaching decisions unanimously dictates some departure from the 'ideal' rule."

215. The constitutionalist approach, Buchanan ([1967] 1999: 221f.) argues, "allows some reconciliation of the purely individualistic and the public interest conception of political order. If the choosing individual is placed in the position of selecting among institutions, among alternative rules of the game, and if he cannot predict with any degree of accuracy his own particular position on subsequent rounds of play, his own private interest will ... lead him to choose rules that will be efficient for the group, taken as a whole. ... This analysis suggests, therefore, that if individuals are appropriately placed in positions where they are required to choose 'constitutionally,' they can be led, by their own self-interest, to act as if they are furthering the general or public interest in some properly meaningful sense."

216. Little (2002: 24): "Progress would surely be inhibited, to the cost of nearly everyone, if all run- of-the-mill investment projects, or changes of policy or practice, whether in the public or private sectors, had to be the subject of a distributional analysis and judgment." – Buchanan (1959: 133, Chapter 10 in this volume): "Any attempt to secure unanimous consent through a compensation scheme for all economic changes would destroy the system."

217. Scitovsky's reference is to Hotelling (1938).

218. See also Samuelson's comment (in: Suzumura 2004: 16): "[T]here is the law of large numbers operating. One invention helps A, another invention helps B; by James Bernoulli's theorem of large numbers, it evens out. The trickle down theory from inequality is bred by the Schumpeterian dynamic process of innovation. The total pie is improved; on the whole and over time, it lifts up everybody. The same tide raises all ships. That is dogmatic faith, but I think it is in the background of intelligent conservatives. John Hicks certainly. His implicit faith is that it will even out. In terms of economic history, there is a lot of truth in that faith."

219. Buchanan ([1988] 2001a: 63): "Individuals may generally agree upon the rules of the game within which ordinary politics takes place, and these agreed upon rules may allow for predicted net gainers and net losers in particularized political choices. The question

of legitimacy or justification shifts directly to the rules, to the constitutional structure, which must remain categorically distinct from the operations of ordinary politics, which is constrained by the rules." – Little (1952: 431, Chapter 18 in this volume) uses a similar language when he states: "Thus an individual will often be prepared to accept a decision which goes against him, because the same decision-making process (or 'procedure,' for short) will be used for making many other decisions between other alternatives, some of which will go in his favor."

220. The qualification "proximate" is a reminder that, as noted before, under less-than-unanimity rules, such as majority rule, "inefficient or nonoptimal outcomes may emerge" (Buchanan [1967] 1999: 289), and that "the political economist, trying to advance hypotheses concerning the existence of 'mutual gains from trade' through the political process, is severely restricted" (Buchanan and Tullock 1962: 94).

221. Nutter (1968: 169, Chapter 36 in this volume): "There is much to be said for encouraging economists to abandon altogether the field of welfare economics as it has developed and to substitute more sophisticated study of alternative economic systems. Let economists raise the question of what system works best ... and not what specific policies are desirable regardless of the system. ... If welfare economics is to be something more than bickering about day-to-day actions on the part of government in carrying out its role in the economy, it must focus on constitutional issues. It must be supplanted, in other words, by political economy in the classical sense."

222. While discussing it in detail would be beyond the scope of the present contribution, it should at least be mentioned that Buchanan's constitutionalism is quite similar to the research program of the Freiburg School of Economics (Vanberg 1998), which also emphasizes that economic policy should be primarily concerned with providing a suitable institutional framework for, instead of directly interfering into, the market process (see Vanberg 1988 and Leipold 1990, Chapter 39 in this volume).

223. Buchanan and Tullock (1962: 23): "Adam Smith and those associated with the movement he represented were partially successful in convincing the public at large that, within the limits of certain general rules of action, the self-seeking activities of the merchant and the moneylender tend to further the general interests of everyone in the community. An acceptable theory of collective choice can perhaps do something similar in pointing the way toward those rules for collective choice-making, the constitution, under which the activities of the political tradesmen can be similarly reconciled with the interests of the members of the social group." – On Adam Smith and "those associated with the movement he represented," Hayek (1948: 12f.) has commented: "The chief concern of the great individualist writers was indeed to find a set of institutions by which man could be induced, by his own choice and from motives which determined his ordinary conduct, to contribute as much as possible to the need of all others."

224. For a more detailed discussion see Vanberg (2005: 37ff., Chapter 41 in this volume).

225. This is implied when Brennan and Buchanan (1985: 26, Chapter 29 in this volume) posit: "Political order must, therefore, be antecedent to economic order."

226. Buchanan taught at the University of Virginia from 1956 to 1968.

227. Buchanan ([1972] 2001: 353): "Stimulated by Frank Knight and, more directly, by Rutledge Vining ... I sensed the possible extensions in the explanatory descriptive power of models for 'rules of games', derived in accordance with some criteria of 'fairness'."

– Buchanan (1992: 13): "Rutledge Vining ... hammered home to all who would listen that economic policy choices are not among allocations or distributions, but are, necessarily, among rules or institutions that generate patterns of allocations and distributions ... Vining took from Knight, and passed along to me, a fully sympathetic listener, the analogy with the choice of rules in ordinary games."

228. In a footnote to a section entitled "The Game Analogy," Vining (1969: 203, fn. 2) states: "In trying to develop this analogy, I have been much influenced by the writings of Frank H. Knight."

229. About the political economist's role Vining (1984: 3, Chapter 37 in this volume) notes: "In the role in which he is familiarly known in the history of the subject, he has practiced his profession as a counselor to legislators in their deliberations upon how well or ill an economic system is working and upon how it might be modified to improve its performance."

230. Vining (1956: 17f.): "The individuals who jointly choose the constraints are the same individuals whose actions are constrained; and they are continually engaged in reviewing the performance of these enactments, just as an individual continually reviews the performance of his personal rules which he has adopted for the guidance of his private action."

231. Vining (1969: 203): "The modifiable entity that men refer to as the economic system is analogous to a game in that it consists, as does a game, of a system of constraining and prescriptive rules and definitions that condition and set limits upon the prudential and means-end choices and decisions exercised by individual members of a population. The designing and enacting of the Federal Reserve Act, the Sherman Anti-Trust Act, the Agricultural Adjustment Act ... are all cases of deliberate alterations of the *economic system* that a people's agents have chosen to make. Each such act constitutes an amendment of existing rules and conditions within the constraints of which individual persons and agencies conduct their private affairs." – Vining (1984: 179, Chapter 37 in this volume): "The true and simple prototype of the theory of our subject is the theory of fair games."

232. Vining (1956: 34, Chapter 8 in this volume): "Now, if the entire society of individuals is regarded as a 'task-oriented group', the objective being well-defined, and if there is presupposed some will or decision-maker who controls the activities of the group directed toward the objective, then the notion of an optimum allocation or efficient use of the manpower and equipment of the society is meaningful. ... This is the confusion that Professor Knight has attempted to clarify. A society of people is not regarded by him as a task-oriented group with a well-defined objective, and no operational meaning can be assigned to the idea of an 'efficient use of a society's resources.' ... The legislative agency of a society of individuals is concerned primarily with the problem of choosing a system of laws and institutions which constrain the choices made by individuals."

233. On the constraints that the participants face in reaching agreement, Vining (1956: 18f) comments: "One can never propose an alteration in an economic system on the explicit grounds that he will gain personally from the alteration – at least he can never do so with any hope that he will be listened to. The proposal must be made on the grounds that the result will be generally more satisfying or else that what now exists is unfair. ... These obligations ... are implied in the idea of a political organization of individuals each of

whom recognizes all of the others as equally free each to act as he wills. To be free to act as one chooses and at the same time to recognize the freedom of others to do likewise can only mean that all participate equally in setting the constraints upon individual action."

234. Buchanan ([1981] 2001: 44): "On many occasions ... I have used the analogy with games since I think this allows us to present the basic distinction most clearly. Consider a poker game. Participants must initially agree on the set of rules that will define the game to be played. This agreed-on set of rules becomes the constitution of the game. Play takes place within these rules .... There are two quite distinct stages or levels of choice involved here, and these choices have quite different features. First, there is the choice of the rules themselves, *constitutional choice*. Second, there is the choice among the strategies of play within the rules that define the game. I call this choice of strategy *post-constitutional choice*."

235. Buchanan (1987: 247, Chapter 38 in this volume): "A simple game analogy illustrates the difference here. The Wicksellian approach concentrates on reform in the rules, which may be in the potential interest of *all* players, as opposed to improvements in the strategies of play for particular players within defined or existing rules."

236. Arrow (1996: xiii) adds: "Under certainty, an action leads to a consequence; but under uncertainty, an action may lead to one of many consequences, which one being uncertain. Hence, choice requires not only the preference among consequences but (uncertain) knowledge of the relation between actions and consequences. Both preferences and judgment are needed."

237. In reference to Bergson's contribution, Arrow ([1951] 1963: 22) notes: "The various arguments of his social welfare function are the components of what I have termed the social state, ... the aim of society then being ..., that it chooses the social state yielding the highest possible social welfare within the environment."

238. Arrow (1969: 223, Chapter 20 in this volume): "The problem of social choice is the aggregation of the multiplicity of individual preference scales about alternative social actions."

239. Arrow explicitly states that "society as a whole will be considered ... to have a social ordering relation for alternative social states" ([1951] 1963: 19), and he expressly speaks of "the choices between pairs of social states made by society" (1950: 335, Chapter 17 in this volume).

240. Sen (1995: 3, Chapter 21 in this volume): "The demands of orderly, overall judgements of 'social welfare' (or the general goodness of states of affairs) were clarified by Abram Bergson (1938), and extensively explored by Paul Samuelson (1947). The concentration was on the need for a real-valued function W of 'social welfare' defined over all the alternative social states ... In the reexamination that followed the Bergson–Samuelson initiative (including the development of social-choice theory as a discipline) the search for the principles underlying a social-welfare function played a prominent role."

241. Vining (1956: 35, Chapter 8 in this volume): "The analytical problem is not that of maximizing or minimizing a particular variable ... Rather, the problem is that of analyzing a process implicit in a sequence of actions by many individuals all taken within a specified system of constraints. The quantitative and qualitative characteristics of this process are among the features that are subjectively considered by the society of individuals, through its legislative procedures, in its evaluation of alternative forms which its laws and

institutions might take."

242. It is significant that, as noted above (section 4.2), in the discussion on Sen's "impossibility theorem" it has been pointed out that the paradox he claims to have identified disappears when the choice situation it is supposed to describe is restated, as it should be, in "game form."

243. Buchanan ([1989] 2001: 269): "A player chooses among strategies available under the rules that define the game; any player's choice will affect the solution that emerges from the choices of all the players, but no player 'chooses' the solution, as such."

244. Buchanan ([1989] 2001: 268): "The complex order of a market economy emerges from a large set of interlinked game-like cooperative interactions between individual sellers and buyers, each of whom maximizes his or her utility in the localized setting of choice. No 'player' in any of these game-like interactions chooses on the basis of an ordinal ranking of 'social states' that describe the possible economy-wide inclusive imputations of goods and services, post-exchange. A 'social choice' among 'social states' (allocations, distributions, value scales) is, therefore, conceptually as well as practicably impossible, so long as any person is allowed to adjust behavior independently in the localized choice setting that is confronted."

245. Buchanan ([1989] 2001: 270): "I have argued that there can be no effective choice among alternate aggregate results, whether the attempt is made individually or collectively. Only the pattern of results is subject to deliberate change and patterns can be changed only through effective changes in structure, i.e., in the set of rules that constrain the exercise of individual choices to be made within the rules."

246. Buchanan (1995: 144, Chapter 40 in this volume): "That which may be chosen or selected in some social choice process is an assignment of rights, … a set of rules that specify the separated domains for the exercise of choice, and action, by the participants." – Acknowledging again Vining's influence, Buchanan (ibid.: 150, fn. 7) notes: "The emphasis that the necessary object for social choices are sets of rules has long been central to the work of my former colleague Rutledge Vining (1984)."

247. Buchanan (1987: 247, Chapter 38 in this volume): "There is no criterion through which policy may be directly evaluated. An indirect evaluation may be based on some measure of the degree to which the political process facilitates the translation of expressed individual preferences into observed political outcomes."

248. Buchanan (1959: 134, Chapter 10 in this volume): "Whereas the 'social welfare function' approach searches for a criterion independent of the choice process, presumably with a view toward influencing the choice, the alternative approach evaluates results only in terms of the choice process itself." – Sugden (1981: 11) comments on Arrow's definition of "social states": "The important omission from this kind of definition of an end state is any description of how it was brought about, or any specification of the processes by which one feasible end state might be substituted for another."

249. Sen (1997: 24, Chapter 22 in this volume): "The philosophical approach underlying social choice theory has strong consequentialist sympathies. Individual preferences are defined over the space of social states, the exercise of aggregation concentrates on social states, and decisions about policies, institutions, rules and so on are seen in terms of appraisal for the states they generate."

250. On the "recent attack" Sen (1997: 24, Chapter 22 in this volume) notes: "The procedural

approach which has been most explored in characterizing liberty was initiated, through libertarianism, by Robert Nozick (1973, 1974) and has been developed, in terms of 'game forms' by Gärdenfors (1981), Sugden (1981, 1985), and Gaertner, Pattanaik and Suzumura (1992), among others."

251. Sen (1997: 24, Chapter 22 in this volume) notes that "a purist position" has been taken by Robert Sugden, who, in turn, comments on the issue: "A liberal who attaches importance to individuals' rights will not be happy with the idea that only end states matter and that the processes by which these end states are reached are of no significance. ... However I do not think that the end state model is entirely anti-liberal. At least one important liberal tenet, that of individualism, can be expressed within the conventions of the model. That is, one can express the view that how far a particular end state is good for society depends entirely on how far it is good for the individuals who make up the society. ... In what I shall call the *procedural model of public choice*, the problem is to choose a procedure or constitution. Value judgements express beliefs not about the relative merits of different end states but about the relative merits of procedures."

252. There would be no reason for Buchanan to object to Sen's (1997: 25, Chapter 22 in this volume) statement: "It is implausible that rights and procedures would be acceptable in actual societies irrespective of what they yield and how people think of what has been yielded." – As Buchanan (1977: 294) expressly says: "Of course, in choosing rules upon which they might conceivably agree, persons will necessarily examine the predicted working properties of alternatives."

253. Under the heading "The Consequent Good or the Antecedent Freedom?" Sen (1985: 2) contrasts "instrumental" defenses of the market "in terms of the goodness of the *results* achieved" (ibid.) with defenses in terms of the "freedom to choose" as a fundamental value (ibid.: 3). In suggesting that the "rights-based 'procedural' view" (ibid.: 4) is about defending markets in terms of the right to choose *within* markets, Sen misses the essential point of Buchanan's distinction between the legitimization of markets by individuals' agreement to the rules that constitute them, and the fact that such agreement may be rationally based on the "goodness" of expected results.

254. As Harsanyi (1958: 306) notes in reference to hypothetical imperatives: "[T]hey must make reference to the addressee's ends to have any prospect of being effective."

255. Sen (2010: 32f.): "The informational foundation of modern social choice theory relates closely to the basic democratic conviction that social judgements and public decisions must depend, in some transparent way, on individual preferences. ... The pioneers of modern social choice theory were guided by their firm conviction that every member of a collectivity must, in principle, count in the decisions of that collectivity. ... Since contemporary social choice theory, pioneered by Arrow, emphatically shares this foundational democratic value, the discipline has continued to be loyal to this basic informational presumption."

256. Buchanan (1975: 2): "The approach must be democratic, which in this sense is merely a variant of the definitional norm of individualism."

257. Vining (1984: 3, Chapter 37 in this volume): "In his most characteristic role as practitioner, the economist is a specialist advisor to legislators and citizens in a legislative frame of mind. The advising of business firms and other administrative organizations or agencies with well-defined ends to attain is an altogether different activity."

258. Whatever else political agents may aim at, gaining and staying in office is the necessary precondition for achieving such other aims through the political process.
259. Bergson (1954: 242): "I have been assuming that the concern of welfare economics is to counsel individual citizens generally. If a public official is counseled, it is on the same basis as any other citizen. In every instance reference is made to some ethical values, which are appropriate for counseling of the individual in question. In all this, I am only expressing the intent of welfare economics generally; or if this is not the intent, I think it should be."
260. Mishan ([1973] 2011: 33): "The social welfare function ... remains a pleasing and nebulous abstraction. It cannot be translated into practical guidance for economic policy. ... Although one can always claim that 'useful insights' have emerged from the attempt to construct theoretical welfare functions, the belief that they can ever be translated into useful economic advice is chimerical."
261. Buchanan ([1982] 2001: 53): "'Economic theory,' as it emerged and has developed, has been almost entirely devoted to analysis of persons within markets ... Prior to the 'public choice revolution,' there was essentially no comparable theory of the interaction of persons within politics. In the absence of such a theory, persons who act on behalf of the sovereign were implicitly modelled as saints, with the predicted consequences. There was a total loss of the 18th-century wisdom that recognized the necessity of constraints on the agents of government."
262. Buchanan ([1967] 1999: 174f.): "If the analyst chooses to work within the confines of the democratic model, he must commence at the level of the individual citizen-voter, and he is obligated to explain how the choices of this citizen-voter are translated into collective decisions." – Buchanan ([1968] 2000: 4): "Most economists and, I suspect, most political scientists, view government as a potentially benevolent despot, making decisions in the 'general' or 'public' interest, and they consider it their own social function to advise and counsel this despot on, first, the definition of this general interest and, second, on the means of furthering it. ... The role of the social scientist who adopts broadly democratic models of the governmental process, who tries to explain and to understand how people do, in fact, govern *themselves*, is a less attractive one than the role that is assumed by the implicit paternalist."
263. Buchanan ([1968] 2000: 4f.): "The social function is not that of improving anything directly; instead, it is that of ... improvements in the political process itself. ... It is wholly beyond his task for the economist to define goals or objectives of the economy or of the government and then to propose measures designed at implementing these goals."

Bibliography

Albert, Hans 1956: "Das Werturteilsproblem im Lichte der logischen Analyse," *Zeitschrift für die Gesamte Staatswissenschaft / Journal of Institutional and Theoretical Economics* 112, 410–439.
Albert, Hans 1965: "Wertfreiheit als methodisches Prinzip: Zur Frage der Notwendigkeit einer normativen Sozialwissenschaft," in: E. Topitsch, *Logik der Sozialwissenschaften*, Köln, Berlin: Kiepenheuer & Witsch, 181–210.

Albert, Hans 1967: "Nationalökonomie und Sozialphilosophie: Zur Kritik des Normativismus in den Sozialwissenschaften," in: *Marktsoziologie und Entscheidungslogik: Ökonomische Probleme in soziologischer Perspektive*, Neuwied am Rhein and Berlin: Luchterhand, 140–174.

Albert, Hans 1979: "The Economic Tradition – Economics as a Research Programme for Theoretical Social Science," in: K. Brunner (ed.), *Economics and Social Institutions*, Boston: Nijhoff, 1–27.

Albert, Hans 1986: *Freiheit und Ordnung – Zwei Abhandlungen zum Problem einer offenen Gesellschaft*, Walter Eucken Institut, Vorträge und Aufsätze 109, Tübingen: J.C.B. Mohr (Paul Siebeck).

Albert, Hans 1998: *Bemerkungen zur Wertproblematik: Von der Bewertung des Sozialprodukts zur Analyse der sozialen Ordnung*, Lectiones Jenenses 15, Jena: Max-Planck-Institut zur Erforschung von Wirtschaftssystemen.

Arrow, Kenneth J. 1951: "Little's Critique of Welfare Economics," *American Economic Review* 41, 923–934.

Arrow, Kenneth J. [1951] 1963: *Social Choice and Individual Values*, 2nd ed., New Haven and London: Yale University Press.

Arrow, Kenneth J. 1963: "Notes on the Theory of Social Choice, 1963," in: *Social Choice and Individual Values*, 2nd ed., New Haven and London: Yale University Press, 92–120.

Arrow, Kenneth J. 1973: "Some Ordinalist-Utilitarian Notes on Rawls' Theory of Justice," *Journal of Philosophy* 70, 245–263.

Arrow, Kenneth J. 1974a: *The Limits of Organization*, New York and London: W.W. Norton.

Arrow, Kenneth J. 1974b: "General Economic Equilibrium: Purpose, Analytic Technique, Collective Choice," *American Economic Review* 64, 253–272.

Arrow, Kenneth J. 1987: "Arrow's Theorem," in: *The New Palgrave Dictionary of Economics*, Vol. 1, London: Palgrave Macmillan, 124–126.

Arrow, Kenneth J. 1994: "Methodological Individualism and Social Knowledge," *American Economic Review* 84, 1–9.

Arrow, Kenneth J. 1996: "Preface," in: K.J. Arrow, E. Colombatto, M. Perlman and Ch. Schmidt (eds.), *The Rational Foundations of Economic Behavior*, New York: St. Martin's Press, xiii–xvii.

Arrow, Kenneth J. 1997: "The Functions of Social Choice Theory," in: K.J. Arrow, A. Sen and K. Suzumura (eds.), *Social Choice Re-examined*, Vol. I, New York: St. Martin's Press, 3–9.

Arrow, Kenneth 2010: "The Classification of Social Choice Propositions," in: K.J. Arrow, A. Sen and K. Suzumura (eds.), *Handbook of Social Choice and Welfare*, Vol. 2, Amsterdam et al.: Elsevier, 24–28.

Arrow, Kenneth J. and J.S. Kelly 2010: "An Interview with Kenneth J. Arrow," in: K.J. Arrow, A. Sen and K. Suzumura (eds.), *Handbook of Social Choice and Welfare*, Vol. 2, Amsterdam et al.: Elsevier, 4–22.

Atkinson, Anthony B. 2009: "Economics as a Moral Science," *Economica* 76, 791–804.

Backhouse, Roger E. 2009: "Robbins and Welfare Economics: A Reappraisal," *Journal of the History of Economic Thought* 32, 474–484.

Backhouse, Roger E. and Steven G. Medema 2009: "On the Definition of Economics," *Journal of Economic Perspectives* 23, 221–233.

Barry, Brian 1986: "Lady Chatterley's Lover and Doctor Fischer's Bomb Party: Liberalism, Pareto Optimality, and the Problem of Objectionable Preferences," in: J. Elster and A. Hylland (eds.), *Foundations of Social Choice Theory*, Cambridge: Cambridge University Press, 11–43.

Baujard, Antoinette 2016: "Welfare Economics," in: G. Faccarello and H.D. Kurz (eds.), *Handbook on the History of Economic Analysis*, Vol. III, Developments in Major Fields of Economics, Cheltenham, UK and Northampton, MA, USA: Edward Elgar, 611–623.

Baumol, William J. 1946: "Community Indifference," *Review of Economic Studies* 14, 44–48.

Bergson, Abram 1938: "A Reformulation of Certain Aspects of Welfare Economics," *Quarterly Journal of Economics* 52, 310–334.

Bergson, Abram 1948: "Social Economics," in: H.S. Ellis (ed.), *A Survey of Contemporary Economics*, Homewood, Illinois: Irwin, 412–448.

Bergson, Abram 1954: "On the Concept of Social Welfare," *Quarterly Journal of Economics* 68, 233–252.

Bergson, Abram 1976: "Social Choice and Welfare Economics under Representative Democracy," *Journal of Public Economics* 6, 171–190.

Black, Duncan 1948: "On the Rationale of Group Decision-Making," *Journal of Political Economy* 56, 23–34.

Borda, Jean-Charles 1781: *Mémoire sur les élections au scrutiny*, Paris.

Buchanan, James M. [1949] 1999: "The Pure Theory of Government Finance: A Suggested Approach," in: *The Logical Foundations of Constitutional Liberty, The Collected Works of James M. Buchanan*, Vol. 1, Indianapolis: Liberty Fund, 119–132.

Buchanan, James M. 1960: *Fiscal Theory and Political Economy: Selected Essays*, Durham: The University of North Carolina Press.

Buchanan, James M. 1962a: "Marginal Notes on Reading Political Philosophy," in: J.M. Buchanan and G. Tullock, *The Calculus of Consent: Logical Foundations of Constitutional Democracy*, Ann Arbor: The University of Michigan Press, 307–322.

Buchanan, James M. 1962b: "The Relevance of Pareto Optimality," *Journal of Conflict Resolution* 6, 341–354.

Buchanan, James M. 1966: "An Individualistic Theory of Political Process," in: D. Easton (ed.), *Varieties of Political Thought*, Englewood Cliffs: Prentice-Hall, 25–37.

Buchanan, James M. [1967] 1999: *Public Finance in Democratic Process: Fiscal Institutions and Individual Choice, The Collected Works of James M. Buchanan*, Vol. 4, Indianapolis: Liberty Fund.

Buchanan, James M. [1968] 1999: *The Demand and Supply of Public Goods, The Collected Works of James M. Buchanan*, Vol. 5, Indianapolis: Liberty Fund.

Buchanan, James M. [1968] 2000: "An Economist's Approach to 'Scientific Politics'," in: *Politics as Public Choice, The Collected Works of James M. Buchanan*, Vol. 13, Indianapolis: Liberty Fund, 3–14.

Buchanan, James M. [1972] 2000: "Toward Analysis of Closed Behavioral Systems," in: *Politics as Public Choice, The Collected Works of James M. Buchanan*, Vol. 13, 25–38.

Buchanan, James M [1972] 2001: "Rawls on Justice as Fairness," in: *Moral Science and Moral Order, The Collected Works of James M. Buchanan*, Vol. 17, 353–359.

Buchanan, James M. 1975: *The Limits of Liberty: Between Anarchy and Leviathan*, Chicago: The University of Chicago Press.

Buchanan, James M. [1975] 2000: "Public Finance and Public Choice," in: *Debt and Taxes, The Collected Works of James M. Buchanan*, Vol. 14, 2–24.

Buchanan, James M. [1975] 2001: "A Contractarian Paradigm for Applying Economic Theory," in: *Choice, Contract, and Constitutions, The Collected Works of James M. Buchanan*, Vol. 16, 79–86.

Buchanan, James M. [1976] 2001: "Methods and Morals in Economics: The Ayres-Knight Discussion," in: *Ideas, Persons, and Events, The Collected Works of James M. Buchanan*, Vol. 19, Indianapolis: Liberty Fund, 123–134.

Buchanan, James M. 1977: "Criteria for a Free Society," in: *Freedom in Constitutional Contract: Perspectives of a Political Economist*, College Station and London: Texas A&M University Press, 287–299.

Buchanan, James M. [1977] 2001: "The Use and Abuse of Contract," in: *Choice, Contract, and Constitutions, The Collected Works of James M. Buchanan*, Vol. 16, Indianapolis: Liberty Fund, 111–123.

Buchanan, James M. [1978] 2000: "From Private Preferences to Public Philosophy: The Development of Public Choice," in: *Politics as Public Choice, The Collected Works of James M. Buchanan*, Vol. 13, Indianapolis: Liberty Fund, 39–56.

Buchanan, James M. 1979: "Retrospect and Prospect," in: *What Should Economists Do?*, Indianapolis: Liberty Press, 279–283.

Buchanan, James M. [1979] 1999: "Natural and Artificial Man," in: *The Logical Foundations of Constitutional Liberty, The Collected Works of James M. Buchanan*, Vol. 1, Indianapolis: Liberty Fund, 246–259.

Buchanan, James M. [1981] 2001: "Constitutional Restrictions on the Power of Government," in: *Choice, Contract, and Constitutions, The Collected Works of James M. Buchanan*, Vol. 16, Indianapolis: Liberty Fund, 42–59.

Buchanan, James M. [1982] 2001: "The Related but Distinct 'Sciences' of Economics and Political Economy," in: *Moral Science and Moral Order, The Collected Works of James M. Buchanan*, Vol. 17, Indianapolis: Liberty Fund, 40–54.

Buchanan, James M. [1983] 2000: "The Public Choice Perspective," in: *Politics as Public Choice, The Collected Works of James M. Buchanan*, Vol. 13, Indianapolis: Liberty Fund, 15–24.

Buchanan, James M. [1984] 1999: "Rights, Efficiency, and Exchange: The Irrelevance of Transaction Costs," in: *The Logical Foundations of Constitutional Liberty, The Collected Works of James M. Buchanan*, Vol. 1, Indianapolis: Liberty Fund, 260–277.

Buchanan, James M. [1985] 2001: "Political Economy and Social Philosophy," in: *Moral Science and Moral Order, The Collected Works of James M. Buchanan*, Vol. 17, Indianapolis: Liberty Fund, 235–250.

Buchanan, James M. [1987] 2001: "Constitutional Economics," in: *Choice, Contract, and Constitutions, The Collected Works of James M. Buchanan*, Vol. 16, Indianapolis: Liberty Fund, 3–14.

Buchanan, James M. [1988] 2001a: "Contractarian Political Economy and Constitutional Interpretation," in: *Choice, Contract, and Constitutions, The Collected Works of James M. Buchanan*, Vol. 16, Indianapolis: Liberty Fund, 60–75.

Buchanan, James M. [1988] 2001b: "Economists and the Gains-from-Trade," in: *Ideas, Persons, and Events, The Collected Works of James M. Buchanan*, Vol. 19, Indianapolis:

Liberty Fund, 135–152.

Buchanan, James M. 1989: "Rational Choice Models in the Social Sciences," in: *Explorations into Constitutional Economics*, College Station: Texas A&M University Press, 37–50.

Buchanan, James M. [1989] 1991: "The Economy as a Constitutional Order," in: *The Economics and Ethics of Constitutional Order*, Ann Arbor: The University of Michigan Press, 29–41.

Buchanan, James M. [1989] 2001: "On the Structure of an Economy," in: *Federalism, Liberty, and the Law, The Collected Works of James M. Buchanan*, Vol. 18, Indianapolis: Liberty Fund, 263–275.

Buchanan, James M. 1990: "The Domain of Constitutional Economics," *Constitutional Political Economy* 1, 1–18.

Buchanan, James M. [1991] 1999: "The Foundations of Normative Individualism," in: *The Logical Foundations of Constitutional Liberty, The Collected Works of James M. Buchanan*, Vol. 1, Indianapolis: Liberty Fund, 281–291.

Buchanan, James M. 1992: *Better than Plowing and Other Personal Essays*, Chicago: The University of Chicago Press.

Buchanan, James M. 1993: "How Can Constitution Be Designed So That Politicians Who Seek to Serve 'Public Interest' Can Survive and Prosper," *Constitutional Political Economy* 4, 1–6.

Buchanan, James M. [1995/96] 2001: "Federalism and Individual Sovereignty," in: *Federalism, Liberty, and the Law, The Collected Works of James M. Buchanan*, Vol. 18, Indianapolis: Liberty Fund, 79–89.

Buchanan, James M. and Roger D. Congleton 1998: *Politics by Principle, not Interest: Towards Nondiscriminatory Democracy*, Cambridge: Cambridge University Press.

Buchanan, James M. and Marilyn R. Flowers 1987: *The Public Finances: An Introductory Textbook*, 6th ed., Homewood, Illinois: Irwin.

Buchanan, James M. and Gordon Tullock 1962: *The Calculus of Consent*, Ann Arbor: The University of Michigan Press.

Chipman, John S. and James C. Moore 1978: "The New Welfare Economics 1939–1975," *International Economic Review* 19, 547–584.

Condorcet, Jean-Antoine-Nicolas 1785: *Essai sur l'application de l'analyse à la probabilité des décisions rendues à la pluralité des voix*, Paris.

Farrell, M.J. 1976: "Liberalism in the Theory of Social Choice," *Review of Economic Studies* 43, 3–10.

Frisch, Ragnar 1959: "On Welfare Theory and Pareto Regions," *International Economic Papers* 9, 39–92.

Gärdenfors, Peter 1981: "Rights, Games and Social Choice," *Nous* 15, 341–356.

Gaertner, Wulf, Prasanta K. Pattanaik and Kotaro Suzumura 1992: "Individual Rights Revisited," *Economica* (New Series) 59, 161–177.

Georgescu-Roegen, Nicholas 1971: *The Entropy Law and the Economic Process*, Cambridge, MA and London: Harvard University Press.

Graaff, J. de V. [1963] 1968: *Theoretical Welfare Economics*, with a Foreword by Paul A. Samuelson, Cambridge: Cambridge University Press.

Gul, F. and W. Pesendorfer 2008: "The Case for Mindless Economics," in: A. Chaplin and A. Schotter (eds.), *The Foundations of Positive and Normative Economics*, London: Oxford

University Press, 3–39.

Hamlin, Allan P. 1991: "Procedural Individualism and Outcome Individualism," in: J.C. Wood and R.N. Woods (eds.), *Friedrich A. Hayek: Critical Assessments*, Vol. IV, London: Routledge, 16–29.

Hands, D. Wade 2013: "Mark Blaug on the Normativity of Welfare Economics," *Erasmus Journal for Philosophy and Economics* 6, 1–25.

Harrod, Roy F. 1938: "Scope and Method of Economics," *Economic Journal* 48, 383–412.

Harsanyi, John C. 1953: "Cardinal Utility in Welfare Economics and in the Theory of Risk-Taking," *Journal of Political Economy* 61, 434–435.

Harsanyi, John C. 1955: "Cardinal Welfare, Individualistic Ethics, and Interpersonal Comparisons of Utility," *Journal of Political Economy* 63, 309–321.

Harsanyi, John C. 1958: "Ethics in Terms of Hypothetical Imperatives," *Mind* LXVII, 305–316.

Harsanyi, John C. 1969: "Cardinal Welfare, Individualistic Ethics, and Interpersonal Comparisons of Utility," in: Kenneth J. Arrow and Tibor Scitovsky (eds.), *Readings in Welfare Economics*, London: George Allen, 46–59.

Harsanyi, John C. 1977a: "Bargaining-Equilibrium Analysis: A New Approach to Game Theory and the Analysis of Social Behavior," in: *Rational Behavior and Bargaining Equilibrium in Games and Social Situations*, Cambridge: Cambridge University Press, 3–15.

Harsanyi, John C. 1977b: "Morality and Social Welfare: A Constructive Approach," in: *Rational Behavior and Bargaining Equilibrium in Games and Social Situations*, Cambridge: Cambridge University Press, 49–83.

Harsanyi, John C. [1977] 1982: "Morality and the Theory of Rational Behavior," in: A. Sen and B. Williams (eds.), *Utilitarianism and Beyond*, Cambridge: Cambridge University Press, 39–62.

Harsanyi, John C. 1998: "A Preference-Based Theory of Well-Being and a Rule-Utilitarian Theory of Morality," in: W. Leinfellner and E. Köhler (eds.), *Game Theory, Experience, Rationality*, Dordrecht, Boston, London: Kluwer Academic Publishers, 285–300.

Hausman, Daniel M. and Michael S. McPherson 1996: *Economic Analysis and Moral Philosophy*, Cambridge: Cambridge University Press.

Hayek, F.A. 1948: *Individualism and Economic Order*, Chicago: The University of Chicago Press.

Hayek, F.A. 1967: "The Economy, Science and Politics," in: *Studies in Philosophy, Politics and Economics*, Chicago: The University of Chicago Press, 251–269.

Hayek, F.A. 1976: The *Mirage of Social Justice*, Vol. 2 of Law, Legislation and Liberty, London and Henley: Routledge & Kegan Paul.

Hennipman, Pieter 1992: "The Reasoning of a Great Methodologist: Mark Blaug on the Nature of Paretian Welfare Economics," *De Economist* 140, 413–445.

Hicks, John R. 1941: "The Rehabilitation of Consumers' Surplus," *Review of Economic Studies* 8, 108–116.

Hicks, John R. 1975: "The Scope and Status of Welfare Economics," *Oxford Economic Papers* 27, 307–326.

Hotelling, Harold 1938: "The General Welfare in Relation to Problems of Taxation and of Railway and Utility Rates," *Econometrica* 6, 242–269.

Hutt, William H. [1936] 1990: "Consumers' Sovereignty," Chapter XVI of *Economists and the Public*, New Brunswick and London: Transaction Publishers, 257–272.

Jevons, William Stanley [1871] 1965: *The Theory of Political Economy*, New York: A.M. Kelley.

Just, Richard E., Darrell L. Hueth and Andrew Schmitz 2004: *The Welfare Economics of Public Policy: A Practical Approach to Project and Policy Evaluation*, Cheltenham, UK and Northampton, MA, USA: Edward Elgar.

Kaldor, Nicolas 1939: "Welfare Propositions of Economics and Interpersonal Comparisons of Utility," *Economic Journal* 49, 549–552.

Kleinewefers, Henner 2008: *Einführung in die Wohlfahrtsökonomie: Theorie – Anwendung – Kritik*, Stuttgart: Kohlhammer.

Knight, Frank H. 1940: "What Is Truth in Economics?" *Journal of Political Economy* 48, 1–32.

Knight, Frank H. [1942] 1982: "Science, Philosophy, and Social Procedure," in: *Freedom and Reform: Essays in Economics and Social Philosophy*, Indianapolis: Liberty Press, 244–267.

Knight, Frank H. [1946] 1982: "The Sickness of Liberal Society," in: *Freedom and Reform: Essays in Economics and Social Philosophy*, Indianapolis: Liberty Press, 440–478.

Lange, Oscar 1942: "The Foundations of Welfare Economics," *Econometrica* 10, 215–228.

Little, I.M.D. 1957: *A Critique of Welfare Economics*, 2nd ed., Oxford: Clarendon Press.

Little, I.M.D. 2002: *Ethics, Economics, and Politics: Principles of Public Policy*, London: Oxford University Press.

Marshall, Alfred [1890] 2014: *Principles of Economics*, London: Palgrave Macmillan.

Mill, John Stuart [1844] 2006: "Essays on Some Unsettled Questions of Political Economy," in: *Essays on Economics and Society, Collected Works of John Stuart Mill*, Vol. IV, Indianapolis: Liberty Fund, 229–339.

Mishan, E.J. 1960: "A Survey of Welfare Economics, 1939–59," *Economic Journal* 70, 197–256.

Mishan, E.J. [1973] 2011: "Welfare Criteria: The Resolution of a Paradox," in: *Economic Efficiency and Social Welfare: Selected Essays on Fundamental Aspects of the Economic Theory of Social Welfare*, London: Routledge, 33–45.

Mishan, E.J. 1980: "The New Welfare Economics: An Alternative View," *International Economic Review* 21, 691–705.

Mueller, Dennis C. 2001: "The Importance of Uncertainty in a Two-Stage Theory of Constitutions," *Public Choice* 108, 223–258.

Müller, Christian 2002: "The Methodology of Contractarianism in Economics," *Public Choice* 113, 465–483.

Myrdal, Gunnar [1922] 1953: *The Political Element in the Development of Economic Theory*, Translated from the German by Paul Streeten, London: Routledge & Kegan Paul.

Ng, Yew-Kwang 1975: "Bentham or Bergson? Finite Sensibility, Utility Functions and Social Welfare Functions," *Review of Economic Studies* 42, 545–569.

Ng, Yew-Kwang 1979: *Welfare Economics: Introduction and Development of Basic Concepts*, London: Macmillan.

Nozick, Robert 1973: "Distributive Justice," *Philosophy & Public Affairs* 3, 45–126.

Nozick, Robert 1974: *Anarchy, State, and Utopia*, New York: Basic Books.

Pareto, Vilfredo [1911] 1955: "Mathematical Economics," *International Economic Papers*, No. 5, 58–102.

Pareto, Vilfredo [1916] 1935: *The Mind and Society: A Treatise on General Sociology*, New York: Harcourt, Brace and Company.

Peacock, Alan T. and Charles K. Rowley 1972: "Pareto Optimality and the Political Economy of Liberalism," *Journal of Political Economy* 80, 476–490.

Pigou, A.C. [1920] 1932: *The Economics of Welfare*, 4th ed., London: Macmillan.

Pigou, A.C. 1951: "Some Aspects of Welfare Economics," *American Economic Review* 41, 287–302.

Pollack, Robert A. 1979: "Bergson–Samuelson Social Welfare Functions and the Theory of Social Choice," *Quarterly Journal of Economics* 93, 73–90.

Posner, Richard A. 1979a: "The Ethical and Political Basis of the Efficiency Norm in Common Law Adjudication," *Hofstra Law Review* 8, 487–507.

Posner, Richard A. 1979b: "Utilitarianism, Economics, and Legal Theory," *Journal of Legal Studies* 8, 103–140.

Radomysler, A. 1946: "Welfare Economics and Economic Policy," *Economica* (New Series) 13, 190–204.

Rawls, John 1963: "Constitutional Liberty and the Theory of Justice," in: C.J. Friedrich and J.W. Chapman (eds.), *Justice*, New York: Atherton Press, 98–125.

Rawls, John 1971: *A Theory of Justice*, Cambridge, MA: Harvard University Press.

Rawls, John [1985] 1999: "Justice as Fairness: Political not Metaphysical," in: S. Freeman (ed.), *Collected Papers*, Cambridge, MA: Harvard University Press, 388–414.

Rawls, John 2001: *Justice as Fairness: A Restatement*, edited by E. Kelly, Cambridge, MA: Harvard University Press.

Robbins, Lionel 1932: *An Essay on the Nature and Significance of Economic Science*, London: Macmillan.

Robbins, Lionel 1938: "Interpersonal Comparison of Utility: A Comment," *Economic Journal* 48, 635–641.

Rothbard, M.N. 1956: "Toward a Reconstruction of Utility and Welfare Economics," in: M. Sennholz (ed.), *On Freedom and Free Enterprise: Essays in Honor of Ludwig von Mises*, Princeton: D. van Nostrand, 224–262.

Rowley, Charles K. and Alan T. Peacock 1975: *Welfare Economics: A Liberal Restatement*, London: Martin Robertson.

Samuelson, Paul A. 1947: *Foundations of Economic Analysis*, Cambridge: Harvard University Press.

Samuelson, Paul A. 1954: "The Pure Theory of Public Expenditure," *Review of Economics and Statistics* 36, 387–389.

Samuelson, Paul A. 1956: "Social Indifference Curves," *Quarterly Journal of Economics* LXX, 1–22.

Samuelson, Paul A. 1958: "Review of J. de V. Graaf, Theoretical Welfare Economics", *Economic Journal* 68, 539–541.

Samuelson, Paul A. 1967: "Arrow's Mathematical Politics," in: S. Hook (ed.), *Human Values and Economic Policy: A Symposium*, New York: New York University Press, 41–51.

Samuelson, Paul A. 1968: "Foreword," in: J. de V. Graaff, *Theoretical Welfare Economics*, Cambridge: Cambridge University Press, vii–viii.

Samuelson, Paul A. 1977: "Reaffirming the Existence of 'Reasonable' Bergson–Samuelson Social Welfare Functions," *Economica* 44, 81–88.

Samuelson, Paul A. 1981: "Bergsonian Welfare Economics," in: St. Rosefielde (ed.), *Economic Welfare and the Economics of Soviet Socialism: Essays in Honor of Abram Bergson*, Cambridge: Cambridge University Press, 223–266.

Samuelson, Paul A. 1983: *Foundations of Economic Analysis – Enlarged Edition*, Cambridge, MA and London: Harvard University Press.

Samuelson, Paul 2004: *Abraham Bergson 1914–2003, A Biographical Memoir*, Washington, DC: The National Academies Press.

Scitovsky, Tibor 1941: "A Note on Welfare Propositions in Economics," *Review of Economic Studies* 9, 77–88.

Sen, Amartya 1970: "The Impossibility of a Paretian Liberal," *Journal of Political Economy* 78, 152–157.

Sen, Amartya 1976: "Liberty, Unanimity and Rights," *Economica* 43, 217–245.

Sen, Amartya 1979a: "Utilitarianism and Welfarism," *Journal of Philosophy* LXXXVI, 463–489.

Sen, Amartya 1979b: "Personal Utilities and Public Judgement: Or What's Wrong with Welfare Economics," *Economic Journal* 89, 537–558.

Sen, Amartya 1983: "Liberty and Social Choice," *Journal of Philosophy* LXXX, 5–28.

Sen, Amartya 1985: "The Moral Standing of the Market," *Social Philosophy and Policy* 2, 1–19.

Sen, Amartya 1986: "Foundations of Social Choice Theory: An Epilogue," in: John Elster and Aanund Hylland (eds.), *Foundations of Social Choice Theory*, Cambridge: Cambridge University Press, 213–248.

Sen, Amartya 1987: "Social Choice," in: *The New Palgrave Dictionary of Economics*, Vol. 4, London: Palgrave Macmillan, 382–393.

Sen, Amartya 1996: "Welfare Economics and Two Approaches to Rights," in: José Casas Pardo and Friedrich Schneider (eds.), *Current Issues in Public Choice*, Cheltenham, UK and Northampton, MA, USA: Edward Elgar, 21–39.

Sen, Amartya 1999: "The Possibility of Social Choice," *American Economic Review* 89, 349–378.

Sen, Amartya 2010: "The Informational Basis of Social Choice," in: K.J. Arrow, A. Sen and K. Suzumura (eds.), *Handbook of Social Choice and Welfare*, Vol. 2, Amsterdam et al.: Elsevier, 29–46.

Sen, Amartya and Bernard Williams 1982: "Introduction: Utilitarianism and Beyond," in: A. Sen and B. Williams (eds.), *Utilitarianism and Beyond*, Cambridge: Cambridge University Press, 1–21.

Senior, Nassau William 1827: *An Introductory Lecture on Political Economy*, London: J. Mawman.

Senior, Nassau William 1836: *An Outline of the Science of Political Economy*, London: W. Clowes and Sons.

Simons, Henry C. [1936] 1948: "Rules versus Authorities in Monetary Policy," in: *Economic Policy for a Free Society*, Chicago: The University of Chicago Press, 160–182.

Smith, Adam [1776] 1981: *An Inquiry into the Nature and Causes of the Wealth of Nations*, Indianapolis: Liberty Classic (reprint of the Oxford University edition of 1976).

Sugden, Robert 1978: "Social Choice and Individual Liberty," in: M. Artis and A.R. Nobay (eds.), *Contemporary Economic Analysis*, London: Croom Helm, 243–267.

Sugden, Robert 1981: *The Political Economy of Public Choice: An Introduction to Welfare Economics*, Oxford: Martin Robertson.

Sugden, Robert 1985: "Liberty, Preference, and Choice," *Economics and Philosophy* 1, 213–229.

Sugden, Robert 1993: "Welfare, Resources, and Capabilities: A Review of Inequality Reexamined by Amartya Sen," *Journal of Economic Literature* XXXI, 1947–1962.

Sugden, Robert 2004: "The Opportunity Criterion: Consumer Sovereignty without the Assumption of Coherent Preferences," *American Economic Review* 94, 1014–1033.

Sugden, Robert and Albert Weale 1979: "A Contractual Reformulation of Certain Aspects of Welfare Economics," *Economica* 46, 111–123.

Suzumura, Kotaro 1996: "Welfare, Rights, and Social Choice Procedure: A Perspective," *Analyse and Kritik* 18, 20–37.

Suzumura, Kotaro 1999: "Paretian Welfare Judgements and Bergsonian Social Choice," *Economic Journal* 109, 204–220.

Suzumura, Kotaro 2000: "Welfare Economics beyond Welfarist-Consequentialism," *Japanese Economic Review* 51, 1–32.

Suzumura, Kotaro 2004: *An Interview with Paul Samuelson: Welfare Economics, "Old" and "New", and Social Choice Theory*, COE/RES Discussion Paper Series, No. 37, Tokyo: Graduate School of Economics and Institute of Economic Research, Hitotsubashi University.

Suzumura, Kotaro 2010: "Welfarism, Individual Rights, and Procedural Fairness," in: K.J. Arrow, A. Sen and K. Suzumura (eds.), *Handbook of Social Choice and Welfare*, Vol. 2, Amsterdam et al.: Elsevier, 605–685.

Tintner, Gerhard 1946: "A Note on Welfare Economics," *Econometrica* 14, 69–78.

Van den Doel, Hans and Ben Van Velthoven 1993: *Democracy and Welfare Economics*, Cambridge: Cambridge University Press.

Van den Hauwe, Ludwig 1999: "Public Choice, Constitutional Political Economy and Law and Economics," in: B. Bouckaert and G. De Geest (eds.), *Encyclopedia of Law and Economics*, Vol. 1, Cheltenham, UK and Northampton, MA, USA: Edward Elgar, 603–659.

Vanberg, Viktor J. 1988: "'Ordnungstheorie' as Constitutional Economics: The German Conception of a 'Social Market Economy'," *ORDO* 39, 17–31.

Vanberg, Viktor J. [1988] 1994: "Morality and Economics: De moribus est disputandum," in: *Rules and Choice in Economics*, London: Routledge, 41–59, 245–249.

Vanberg, Viktor J. 1992: "Organizations as Constitutional Systems," *Constitutional Political Economy* 3, 223–253.

Vanberg, Viktor J. 1998: "Freiburg School of Law and Economics," in: Peter Newman (ed.), *The New Palgrave Dictionary of Economics and the Law*, Vol. 2, 172–179.

Vanberg, Viktor J. 2003: "Citizens' Sovereignty, Constitutional Commitments, and Renegotiation: Original versus Continuing Contract," in: A. Breton, G. Galeotti, P. Salmon and R. Wintrobe (eds.), *Rational Foundations of Democratic Politics*, Cambridge: Cambridge University Press, 198–221.

Vanberg, Viktor J. 2004: "The Status Quo in Contractarian-Constitutionalist Perspective,"

Constitutional Political Economy 15, 153–170.

Vanberg, Viktor J. 2007: "Democracy, Citizen Sovereignty and Constitutional Economics," in: José Casas Pardo and Pedro Schwartz (eds.), *Public Choice and the Challenges of Democracy*, Cheltenham, UK and Northampton, MA, USA: Edward Elgar, 101–120.

Vanberg, Viktor J. 2008: "On the Economics of Moral Preferences," *American Journal of Economics and Sociology* 67, 605–628.

Vanberg, Viktor J. 2011: "Consumer Welfare, Total Welfare and Economic Freedom – on the Normative Foundations of Competition Policy," in: J. Drexl, W. Kerber and R. Podzun (eds.), *Competition Policy and the Economic Approach: Foundations and Limitations*, Cheltenham, UK and Northampton, MA, USA: Edward Elgar, 44–71.

Vanberg, Viktor J. 2012: "Methodological and Normative Individualism in The Calculus," *Public Choice* 152, 381–388.

Vanberg, Viktor J. 2014: "James M. Buchanan's Contractarianism and Modern Liberalism," *Constitutional Political Economy* 25, 18–38.

Vanberg, Viktor J. and James M. Buchanan 1989: "Interests and Theories in Constitutional Choice," *Journal of Theoretical Politics* 1, 49–62.

Vanberg, Viktor J. and James M. Buchanan 1991: "Constitutional Choice, Rational Ignorance and the Limits of Reason," *Jahrbuch für Neue Politische Ökonomie*, Vol. 10, Tübingen: Siebeck Mohr, 61–78.

Varian, Hal R. 1975: "Distributive Justice, Welfare Economics, and the Theory of Fairness," *Philosophy & Public Affairs* 4, 223–247.

Viner, Jacob 1937: *Studies in the Theory of International Trade*, New York and London: Harper.

Vining, Rutledge 1956: *Economics in the United States of America: A Review and Interpretation of Research*, Paris: UNESCO.

Vining, Rutledge 1969: "On Two Foundation Concepts of the Theory of Political Economy," *Journal of Political Economy* 77, 199–218.

Vining, Rutledge 1984: *On Appraising the Performance of an Economic System*, Cambridge: Cambridge University Press.

Walras, Léon [1874] 1984: *Elements of Pure Economics or The Theory of Social Wealth*, translated by William Jaffé. Philadelphia, PA: Orion Editions.

Weale, Albert 1992: "Social Choice," in: S. Hargreaves Heap, M. Hollis, B. Lyons, R. Sugden and A. Weale, *The Theory of Choice: A Critical Guide*, Oxford and Cambridge, MA: Blackwell, 199–216.

Recommended Reading

10.   James M. Buchanan (1959), 'Positive Economics, Welfare Economics, and Political Economy', *Journal of Law and Economics*, 2, October, 124–38

11.   Abram Bergson (1966), 'On Social Welfare Once More', in *Essays in Normative Economics*, Part I, Chapter 3, Cambridge, MA, USA: The Belknap Press of Harvard University Press, 51–77

12.   John Rawls ([1971] 1999), 'Classical Utilitarianism' and 'Some Related Contrasts', in *A Theory of Justice: Revised Edition*, Chapter 1, Sections 5 and 6, Cambridge, MA, USA: The Belknap Press of Harvard University Press, 19–30

13.   Lionel Robbins (1981), 'Economics and Political Economy', *American Economic Review: Papers and Proceedings*, 71 (2), May, 1–10

14.   John C. Harsanyi (1988), 'Assessing Other People's Utilities', in Bertrand R. Munier (ed.), *Risk, Decision and Rationality*, Dordrecht, Holland: D. Reidel Publishing Company, 127–38

15.   Anthony B. Atkinson (2011), 'The Restoration of Welfare Economics', *American Economic Review: Papers and Proceedings*, 101 (3), May, 157–61

16.   Viktor J. Vanberg (2014), 'Evolving Preferences and Welfare Economics: The Perspective of Constitutional Political Economy', *Jahrbücher für Nationalökonomie und Statistik*, 234 (2–3), April, 328–49

B   **Social Choice Theory: From Individual Preferences to Social Orderings**

17.   Kenneth J. Arrow (1950), 'A Difficulty in the Concept of Social Welfare', *Journal of Political Economy*, 58 (4), August, 328–46

18.   I. M. D. Little (1952), 'Social Choice and Individual Values', *Journal of Political Economy*, 60 (5), October, 422–32

19.   James M. Buchanan (1954), 'Social Choice, Democracy, and Free Markets', *Journal of Political Economy*, 62 (2), April, 114–23

20.   Kenneth J. Arrow (1969), 'Values and Collective Decision-making', in Peter Laslett and W.G. Runciman (eds), *Philosophy, Politics and Society: Third Series*, Oxford, UK: Basil Blackwell, 215–32

21.   Amartya Sen (1995), 'Rationality and Social Choice', *American Economic Review*, 85 (1), March, 1–24

32.   Georg Vanberg and Viktor Vanberg (2017), 'Contractarian Perspectives in Law and
        Economics', in Francesco Parisi (ed.), T*he Oxford Handbook of Law and
        Economics: Volume 1, Methodology and Concepts*, Chapter 12, Oxford, UK and
        New York, NY, USA: Oxford University Press, 246–67

B   Constitutionalism: Rules as Objects of Choice

33.   F. A. Hayek (1960), 'Economic Policy and the Rule of Law', in *The Constitution of
        Liberty*, Chapter 15, Chicago, IL, USA: University of Chicago Press, 220–33, notes

34.   James M. Buchanan and Gordon Tullock (1962), 'A Generalized Economic Theory
        of Constitutions', in *The Calculus of Consent: Logical Foundations of
        Constitutional Democracy*, Part II, Chapter 6, Ann Arbor, MI, USA: University of
        Michigan Press, 63–84

35.   Franz Böhm (1989), 'Rule of Law in a Market Economy', in Alan Peacock and
        Hans Willgerodt (eds), Germany's Social Market Economy: Origins and Evolution,
        Chapter 4, New York, NY, USA: St. Martin's Press, 46–67

36.   G. Warren Nutter (1968), 'Economic Welfare and Welfare Economics', *Journal of
        Economic Issues*, 2 (2), 166–72

37.   Rutledge Vining (1984), 'Three Main Concepts that Inhere in the Circumstances
        Cited' and 'Concluding Remarks upon What an Economic System Is, and the
        Problem of Specifying Norms of the Outcome of Its Working', in *On Appraising
        the Performance of an Economic System*, Chapter 1 and Chapter 6, Cambridge,
        UK: Cambridge University Press, 3–33, 170–81, references

38.   James M. Buchanan (1987), 'The Constitution of Economic Policy', *American
        Economic Review*, 77 (3), June, 243–50

39.   Helmut Leipold (1990), 'Neoliberal Ordnungstheorie and Constitutional
        Economics: A Comparison between Eucken and Buchanan', *Constitutional
        Political Economy*, 1 (1), December, 47–65

40.   James M. Buchanan (1995), 'Individual Rights, Emergent Social States, and
        Behavioral Feasibility', *Rationality and Society*, 7 (2), April, 141–50

41.   Viktor J. Vanberg (2005), 'Market and State: The Perspective of Constitutional
        Political Economy', *Journal of Institutional Economics*, 1 (1), June, 23–49